ARE YOU BEING SERVED YET?

CUSTOMER SERVICE EVOLUTION

Ron Berger

PublishAmerica
Baltimore

© 2006 by Ron Berger.
All rights reserved. No part of this book may be reproduced, stored in a retrieval system or transmitted in any form or by any means without the prior written permission of the publishers, except by a reviewer who may quote brief passages in a review to be printed in a newspaper, magazine or journal.

The pictures included in this book show how these two companies (The William Lyon Company and The Konwiser Corp.), although differing in size, treated their employees. Whether large or small, your employees are also your customers. These pictures were taken by the author/wife and the *Orange County Register* newspaper and used with permission.

First printing

At the specific preference of the author, PublishAmerica allowed this work to remain exactly as the author intended, verbatim, without editorial input.

ISBN: 1-4241-2485-9
PUBLISHED BY PUBLISHAMERICA, LLLP
www.publishamerica.com
Baltimore

Printed in the United States of America

CONTENTS

DEDICATION	5
ACKNOWLEDGMENTS	7
AUTHOR'S NOTE	9
FOREWORD	11
IN THE BEGINNING:	14
THE MILWAUKEE JOURNAL	14
THE US AIR FORCE	18
CIVILIAN LIFE	22
FULL-TIME EMPLOYMENT—BUILDERS:	25
THE BEST	27
THE NEXT BEST	38
THE WORST	48
NEXT WORST	52
HOME TEAM	55
THE 3-P'S OF CUSTOMER SERVICE	63
SIGNS OF BAD CUSTOMER SERVICE	70
TQM—TOTAL QUALITY MANAGEMENT	76
GE—THE GENERAL ELECTRIC COMPANY	79
FORD MOTOR COMPANY	83
ADMIRAL APPLIANCES	87
GATEWAY COMPUTER	90
SOUTHWEST AIRLINES	92
DELL COMPUTER	96
FARMER BOYS	99
NEWS ARTICLES	102
LIP SERVICE	105
BY THE BOOK	108
CUSTOMER TRUST	110
WHO'S RESPONSIBLE?	114
HOW TO CHANGE	117
PERSONNEL	120
TRAINING	123

SUPERVISION	128
MONITORING RESULTS	132
IMPLEMENTING CORRECTIONS	136
REWARDING EXCELLENCE	138
PRESS (*) TO BE IGNORED	142
CONCLUSIONS	147
MISSION STATEMENTS	150

Dedication

I would like to dedicate this book to all the GREAT service personnel I have been associated with during my 41 years in construction. Not everyone I knew fits into this category, but those that did the great service know who I'm talking about.

Also—to those few companies that allowed me to work in this great service atmosphere, I thank you. I will go to my grave thankful for being able to have worked for you.

Four people come to mind as essential personnel in making this part of my life's adventure meaningful and downright fun.

- **Gilda Stern**, who I had the pleasure of working with at several companies, is without a doubt one of the best, all-around, hands-on, dedicated service oriented persons I have ever known. Not only was she a great student, but having grasped the best service phylosphy, she was able to impart it to others. Working at both The Konwiser Corporation and National Builders' Service (Home Team), I will cherish every moment that we worked together to bring better service to our customers.

When writing about good service, The William Lyon Company is the one that had both of these next two people.

- **Dave Coughlin**—Dave was my customer service field manager. He is the one that had the level head when approaching a problem and was the persistant and knowledgable person to carry out solutions. His manner was such that his actions were never questioned, because they were always deemed right. Dave was a great help to me in other departments as well. One hell of a great company man and friend.

- **Cyndy Legowski**—Cyndy was actually my second choice in personnel selection for the customer service manager position in the office. The first choice quit before she started and Cyndy immediately accepted. This was probably one of the best things that I failed at in choosing personnel. Cyndy's ability to work at my brand of service and carry it forward in every respect gained my everlasting gratitude. Without her attitude and dexterity, customer service just wouldn't have been the same. I just know that my first choice wouldn't have been the best choice.

The one bright spot for customer service at the S•R Group was a person who did everything in his power to deliver great service.

- **Dave Cosby** had been on all sides of construction, but customer service was his forte. Without Dave, the entire project in Oakland would have been a total disaster.

Acknowledgments

Again, as in my first book, *The House That Ron Built*, I need to thank my wife Nancy for all the times she had to listen to my ramblings about work. The many times I would come back from a flight to Northern California totally exhausted from battling the stubborn owners of the project as well as the exasperated homeowners. It was so great to be home with her.

The Konwiser Corporation for allowing me to truly begin the customer service part of my career. Although we were mainly dealing with renters, the methods learned were easily carried over to buyers at other companies.

The William Lyon Company was, without a doubt, the Best in the West. Between 1988 and 1992, only the best service could be found at the Central Counties Division of this company. Thanks to the boss—General Lyon—for instituting this phenomenon called great customer service. It was innovating, inspirational and satisfying all at the same time. It was like finally reaching the proverbial light at the end of the tunnel.

Author's Note

When I first started to write this book, I thought the title "The CS *Revolution*" would be appropriate. However, I realized that at the rate customer service was improving, EVOLUTION would be a better word.

Ron

FOREWORD

Customer Service is one of those things that most companies claim they have, but very few understand it. Some even claim they have the best and hire uneducated people to operate it.

Customer Service is actually the easiest thing to perform and most companies treat it as being the hardest. The mindset of most business people is that the main part of a business is selling goods or a service and making a profit. It's true that these need to be accomplished, but how to get people to buy your goods or services may very well depend on the kind of customer service you offer.

I had never given customer service much thought. In fact, I really never heard of it until I had started in the building business and was told—after completing several houses—that now the customer service part starts. What was that?

Looking back on the jobs I had previously, I realized that customer service was involved, but no one talked about it as being a vital part of business. I had never run across anyone that considered customer service important. This was a take it or leave it time and you needed to be thankful for what you got instead of complaining.

My attitudes followed this feeling for many years. Anyone who complained about "my" houses must be off base. How dare they complain about something I put all that hard work into? It was a direct slap in my face and I didn't appreciate it very much.

Having been an air traffic controller in the United States Air Force as well as starting in the construction industry, my method to solving problems was to issue orders. My ego would not allow me to accept blame for anything. My work was above reproach, especially when I put so much effort into being right.

Life has a way of changing a person's mind about things. With some it takes longer than others. I've been taught many lessons in my life. Many of which may have saved my life and others have definitely made my life better. Learning about Customer Service did not come easy and wasn't one of the first to enter my life. It took many years and many tries before the very essence of Customer Service became a staple with me.

Why write a book about Customer Service? Why indeed. What took me over 41 years in the construction industry to learn is still a mystery to a majority of people that desperately need to know about it. Companies come and go. Business's start up and close up. People invest their efforts in making their ideas work and completely forget about the customer.

Most of my efforts have been in the construction industry and builders are what I know best. Not many builders are even willing to talk with the customer to say nothing about listening to one complaining. They hire as many people as necessary to run interference for them so that "personal" contact may be bypassed.

Although I have had other jobs besides construction related, Customer Service is found everywhere—or the lack of it. So—return with me to my earlier life when Customer Service was just being invented.

**CUSTOMER SERVICE IS NOT A SERVICE...
IT'S AN ATTITUDE!**

**CUSTOMER SERVICE DOESN'T COST...
IT PAYS!**

IN THE BEGINNING: The Milwaukee Journal—

In 1948 I started my work experience by delivering *The Milwaukee Journal* every day for about four years. This was an afternoon paper, delivered rain or shine, sun or snow. The Sunday paper was an early morning edition and sometimes would weight up to five pounds apiece. There was always a push to get new customers. They would have us canvas our routes to dig up additional sales. Sometimes you would do this with enthusiasm, but most of the time you would drag your heals and only do what little you could. Why exert all that effort only to be turned down and didn't we do enough already? We work in all kinds of weather, eat the cost when customers didn't pay and generally take verbal abuse when their paper got wet. We had to collect monies from our customers every Saturday in order to pay our paper bill on Sunday. We only made one half-cent per paper for dailies and one-cent for Sundays. When you have, on average, 70 dailies and 80 Sundays you can see that money wasn't the reason you stayed on. Earning less than three dollars per week was still spending money. Of course if you couldn't collect from everyone, that came out of yours. Basically you received what was left over after paying your paper bill. I had one customer that eventually owed me over $25. When I finally found him (he was the ex-mayor and I couldn't stop his paper) and he agreed to pay—I thought I had hit a gold mine.

I became Station Captain, which was the position of paper dispenser, paper stuffer, money collector and dealer deliverer. I was able to get out of school one hour earlier than everyone else so I could get the papers ready for the paperboys. This paid ten dollars a week. Quite an increase, plus most of the work was done inside and out of the weather.

I shared this work with a friend of mine as we both needed spending money. This meant that we each received five dollars per week, just slightly more than what I was making as a paperboy. However, this was a management type job and ranked higher than a lowly paperboy.

One day, the District Supervisor came to town to kick off a new program to sign up new subscribers. Not only did this involve the regular paperboys, but us "management type" workers as well. This was about the lowest blow I could have been dealt. Can you imagine management people going door to door selling newspapers? I was so distraught that my sales pitch came out as a guaranteed rebuff of my efforts. "You don't want to take *The Milwaukee Journal*, do you?" That attitude only proved my point that I was not the one to be doing this. I nearly lost my job because of that and it became one of the first lessons in customer service that I received—although I didn't realize it at the time.

This was also the time in my life when magazine sales were mandatory in every school year to raise extra money for our class. Some years you were lucky and sold a few subscriptions. Some years you couldn't give them away. This was not an affluent town I lived in and many people had trouble paying 30 cents a week for the paper. The pressure always seemed to be on to sell—sell—sell.

The one thing that really stuck with me is getting over my fear of meeting and talking with people. Although the fear never really went away, this early experience certainly helped in my succeeding positions.

I was proud (most of the time) to be associated with *The Milwaukee Journal*. It was and, I believe, still is the largest paper in Wisconsin. Although the name has changed slightly to The *Milwaukee Journal-Sentinel*. *The Milwaukee Sentinel* used to be a rival until they merged a number of years ago. The Journal was a big backer for the Milwaukee sport teams and helped create the feeling that the entire State owned the Packers and the Braves (when they were still in Milwaukee).

The main radio station to service our area was WTMJ which was owned by the newspaper and was listened to by everyone who had the slightest interest in any sports. This fact alone made you feel like you worked for a pretty large and important company. You felt a little pride when you told people you worked for *The Milwaukee Journal*. You had a tendency to overlook the slave labor wages you were making and the impossible working conditions that you were subject to nearly every day.

Their Customer Service to us slaves would be a once a year *Journal Jamboree* that was held in Milwaukee and everyone associated with the paper was invited. Of course you had to qualify for this honor by getting "x" number of new subscriptions. If you didn't the invitation was withdrawn. This was about a two hour show full of circus acts that was presented to honor all the employees, especially the paperboys. After several years in attending, us management type got tired of the elementary level of entertainment and would see what other attractions were available in the big city.

This is how Customer Service used to be handled. It didn't matter that you work hard and faithfully all year, you still had to do more to be eligible for a reward. They didn't realize that we were their customers as well. Many companies have that same attitude today. Their employees are expendable and not considered "customers."

The United States Air Force—

The US Air Force, or for that matter any branch of the military, is not a subject worth studying regarding Customer Service. They are not in the business to please anyone. They are there to carry out their mission—whatever that may be. However, how you treat other personnel still falls under the guidelines of common decency. This, in itself, is a large portion of Customer Service. We do not live in a dictatorship where any kind of order has to be obeyed, like many countries. But, we do not live in a country that has their military run by a democracy either. We could not have the entire country suggest various ways of doing things. There has to be leadership.

Serving in the control tower during my duty in service enlightened me as to how you can provide Customer Service in your daily endeavors. Although I didn't think about it when I was in service, but reflecting on it later, showed that there was something resembling Customer Service. How you talked to pilots and how they talked to you was pretty much written in the manual. But, the tone of voice plus the added phraseology would mean the difference between a pleasant conversation and a strained one.

Every pilot was an officer and every tower operator was an enlisted man and there in was the source of many unpleasant match-ups. How dare enlisted personnel tell an officer what to do? It's unheard of in the military. This occurred a number of times and I was lucky with most of them by having a commanding officer who really stood behind his controllers and put other officers in their place, even the base commander. Our Major was supplying great Customer Service to his troops. There wasn't much that we wouldn't do for him.

The Major left on a 30 day leave and placed his adjutant in charge. We ended up marching and doing KP right up to the time the Major came back. Once he heard what was going on he called a halt to all the "extra stuff" and said that all his boys had to do was their job and do it right. He likened us to true professionals and always listened to our side of the story. Nothing could have been more ego and confidence building than that.

The Sergeant in charge of the tower was also one that would go to bat for you—if he felt you were right. He was tough, but also fair. All of us in the tower felt that we had an unbeatable combination. In fact, I was seriously considering the re-up process, but I didn't quite have the minimum amount of time in to do that. As it turned out, when I did have the required time in, orders from on high came down that said my buddy and I were to report to Saudi Arabia right away. Since we were in England and not even knowing where Saudi Arabia was, we were in a hell of a mess.

We had the qualifications that were needed in Saudi Arabia and there wasn't anything the Major or the Sergeant could do about it to change the orders. My only saving grace was that I hadn't re-upped prior. That was poor Customer Service on the Air Forces' part, but than again, they are not in the Customer Service business.

The big wigs in Saudi Arabia could have used lessons in common sense as well as Customer Service. There weren't any redeeming qualities in any of those "superior" personnel that made life in this sweat box any easier. I think the heat got to them all and fried their brains. It seemed like their big concern was that they had the controls to the air conditioner and you didn't.

The Captain in charge never came up to the tower, had no idea what it was like, never flew a plane and was generally grumpy every time you met. His lackluster leadership ability confirmed my feelings that I couldn't wait now to get out of this man's Air Force.

The Sergeant in charge of the tower was weak as a leader. He couldn't handle any position in the tower without supervision. He would come out saying that you should re-enlist, like he has done, for your own good. I told him that he probably couldn't get a job on the outside and that's the reason he had re-enlisted so many times. He became quite angry, but I'm also sure he saw some truth to it.

Both of these leaders did not represent mentors or even responsible Air Force material. When I realized that there probably were more of these leaders out there I was quite concerned. The difference between England and Saudi Arabia was not the weather, but rather the professionalism of the parties in charge.

The rest of my military time was spent with a mobile squadron out of Tinker AFB in Oklahoma City, Oklahoma. We were sent on temporary duty in Wisconsin and California to facilitate quality air traffic control for the National Guard units at camp. There really wasn't anything to do with Customer Service at these summer camps. The different Guard units would only be there for two weeks and it took that long for our complaints about the rotten food to reach someone that could do something about it.

The Sergeant in charge of the operators was a small, but mighty, African-American who really knew how to work with people. He helped me out several times, as well as others. When my time was getting short, he personally made a pitch for my promotion which carried the day. After having 32 months time in grade for a stripe that only required 12, I finally received it. That's what happens when you get transferred; you go to the bottom of the list again.

This Sergeant, for whom I had great respect, now had to ask the question posed to all short timers; "will you re-enlist?" He knew very well what my plans were, but had to ask. I only wish I could have spent more time with those in England as well as this Sergeant in Oklahoma. Then the Air Force would have been a good bet on making a career in air traffic control.

In a recent newspaper article, it stated that the services were changing their approach to recruiting. During the second year of the second Iraq war, the numbers were declining to maintain our all volunteer armed forces. Although the numbers weren't that low, something needed to be done before it really got to be a problem. Could it be that the services were trying to figure out how to implement some good customer service?

Apparently, they thought if they took in consideration what the new recruit wanted, maybe they would be more excited about joining. I know that this is going to be a stretch for the services, especially when the new recruit wants to joint as a general.

Never let it be said that stones cannot be moved or some things are written in concrete. This proves that ANYTHING can happen if needed.

Civilian Life—

Once out of service, marriage was the next step in Customer Service. Marriage probably played the biggest part in my education in Customer Service. You may not think it had much to do with it, but believe me, it did. You have to learn to live together, work together and help solve each others problems. This doesn't come easy from someone that has an inflated ego. After all—I had been half way around the world and had seen a lot—therefore, I must know a lot. WRONG!

While attending college, my English instructor started giving me some low grades on test papers. This just wasn't right. I was an honor student in high school and just wasn't worthy of low grades. After an unsatisfying discussion with the instructor, I continued to feel that I was, somehow, being singled out for ego busting. Nothing I could do or say solved this problem. After all, it seemed like I was being threatened and someone wanted to take one of the few things I felt I had a good grip on—my ego.

Working part time for Sears Roebuck, I also felt put upon by management. They would shift me all around the store—wherever they needed extra help. I was very seldom left in one department long enough to really get the feel of it and make some commissions. Sales people received a one percent commission on all sales and a four percent commission of Sears brand products. They didn't give you any instructions on how to sell items, only in the filling out of sales slips.

I was in the camera department one night and a couple came up to me and asked about a specific camera as a present. I knew something about cameras and was able to make the sale. Several minutes after the customers left, I was chastised by a regular salesperson for making the sale. "Are you sure that they hadn't talked with a regular salesperson prior to tonight and that the sale should have been theirs?" They couldn't believe that I could have made that sale. What did I know about expensive cameras? Talk about taking the wind out of your sails. Instead of encouraging me on, they basically accused me of stealing sales from someone else. What a blow to my self-esteem.

Another incident occurred in the same department, but in the stationery and typewriter part. I had a couple come in asking if I could give them some clues on what to get their daughter, who was in college, for Christmas. After thinking a moment and without saying a word, I motioned them to follow me as I led them to the typewriters. I typed the familiar sentence that most people learn very early on in their typing education—*"Now is the time for all good men to come to the aid of their country."* They took one look at the paper and bought it. This happened to be one of the first script typewriters available and so novel that it didn't take any selling what-so-ever. No one could have accused me of stealing their customer when I didn't even talk with them.

The people in their personnel department had some experience in Customer Service. One especially, seemed to be very concerned about what you had to say. She was an excellent "dispatcher." She gave you the feeling that your needs came before the stores. Of course they didn't, but that was a great feeling that she was able to impart. This isn't to say that the store was filled with these customer related personnel.

Also at Christmas, my wife and I decided to shop at Sears. Employees received a discount, but we still didn't have enough cash to shop. We were told to apply for credit and then go shopping. It didn't take long to fill out the credit form and we were given a temporary card to get started with. It didn't take us long to round up several gifts and approached the check-out only to be told that we couldn't charge those gifts. We were told that you had to buy a minimum of $50.00 before you could charge. You may not remember, but back in those days' fifty-dollars was a lot of money. We left all the gifts at the register and left the store. What a disappointment. Why didn't they tell us when we applied? It could have saved us a lot of embarrassment and kept their name in a better light with us. It was quite awhile before we shopped there again.

What does all this have to do with Customer Service? Only that you can see that the attitude that is given to others affects the way business is run. Whether you're in a controlled business, like the service or an open business, like Sears, having an understanding how Customer Service works will make all the difference in the world.

Full-Time Employment—
Builders

Working for my first builder brought on the words, Customer Service. Not that it was an overwhelming goal in the company, but maybe something a little more than lip service.

Upon completing several homes and the buyers moved in, I was told that Customer Service would be needed. This was totally foreign to me. What could possibly be wrong with my houses? The new buyers should be thankful that I was the superintendent and everything was perfect. The builder (owner) took care of the walk-through and generally talked the buyers out of complaining about anything. It didn't always work and then I would get the complaint to do something about it.

It was a good thing that I had some knowledge of tools and how things went together because the builder hated to pay extra for anything. I was able to do most of the repairs myself and save the lectures about doing things right the first time. If money had to be spent, it was always called: "after tax dollars" or "money out of pocket." You were always made to feel like you were sticking your hand in the builder's pocket and stealing his money.

Most of the Customer Service complaints had to do with the quality subcontractors that were hired. I tried to always get the best that I knew to get the job, but was overruled many times to keep the costs down. Of course keeping the costs down was a prerequisite on every job. In order to keep the best on the job; I developed standard contracts so that we would know the costs as soon as the job was designed. I would do a take-off for concrete, framing, lumber, electrical, plumbing, sheet metal, windows and roofing. This gave us a pretty good idea what the final costs would be. I would have the other subcontractors bid their part of the job in order to get the full results.

The subcontractors that had a standard contract were assured of getting all our work, as long as their prices remained stable. This went a long way to forming partnerships and gave us a better quality home than ever before. They didn't have to spend time bidding so they were already ahead of the game. We actually had very few call backs. Most call backs generally came from the subcontractors that didn't have a standard contract. Apparently they didn't feel as connected to the house as the others.

Although this first builder was where I first learned about Customer Service doesn't mean that it was really high up the priority ladder and that every other builder I worked for had the same or better attitude towards it. At least this builder had some Customer Service, which can't be said about all the other nine.

The Best—

The best builder for Customer Service, without a doubt, was The William Lyon Company, of Newport Beach, CA, during the period from 1988 to 1992. This was just prior to an economy down-turn and construction went in the dumpster. The middle of 1992 was the time that the banks thought they knew more about building a house than the builder and basically took over many companies. The four years before was the most exciting in the Customer Service field.

I really lucked out by being hired by The William Lyon Company. They were already known as the best builder and to be associated with them was really exciting. Not only were we building a great product, but the name alone was worth a great deal of money. About four months after I arrived as Director of Construction of the North Orange County Division, General Lyon set out to establish a better Customer Service department. He hired specialists to come up with a plan to best represent his feeling that "we are number one, because you are number one with us." General Lyon knew that the customer was the one actually paying the bills and needed to be served on a much higher scale.

Books and manuals were produced and given the classification as the "bible" for Customer Service. Training sessions were scheduled as well as individual help when needed. All this was ordered and blessed by the General himself. We all knew that it couldn't fail if it came from the top.

However, there were quite a few divisions in the company and they all seemed to take the orders slightly different. Just like the service. You could be ordered to dig a hole and one person would dig six inches deep and call it good. Another would go a foot and stop. Yet still another would still be digging when told to stop. All thought they were following the same orders, but the results would be quite different.

Several things were needed to make sure the right results were being obtained. One was that a Customer Service computer program would be needed to keep track of all service requests and how they were handled. The other needed to be a survey which was independent and told us what the buyers really thought. This also meant that our computer program had to be operated fairly, without any padding, so that the two would be comparable. You couldn't have one program say everything was A-OK and the customer surveys complain about everything.

There were three divisions in our company included in the surveys and it was interesting to see how we all faired. Out of the 21 different builder projects being surveyed, my division ranked #2 in all the surveys. The number one builder, whom we never found out, only produced about 50 homes a year compared to our 400 plus. This survey covered all aspects of building and buying a new house. To come out as number two only made us feel like Avis and we needed to try harder. These surveys came out every three months and were really gone over when they arrived.

The other two involved divisions were always seventh or further down the line. They couldn't advance because they were only digging a six inch hole and they figured that was enough. They still stuck with the old school thoughts and were afraid to invest in the new school. Even though the Vice Presidents were all schooled on what the General wanted there was always reasons why advancement couldn't be made. Actually, they didn't care about Customer Service advancement as much as their wanting to stick to the old ways and not change their habits right from the beginning.

Their methods of saving money actually cost more in the end. Hiring contractors that did work that was considered less than best and coupling that with either inexperienced or highly harassed supervision was a disaster just waiting to happen. This usually came to light after the buyer moved in or the first rain storm happened and the calls started flooding in. *You just can not have great Customer Service in the end if the product is designed to fail from the beginning.* Those divisions didn't look at it in that light, but rather that maybe a good sub had gone bad.

Our division didn't only adopt the General's orders in word, but also in spirit. The Lyon Company had built some homes about 17 years before and one day I got a call from one of those owners. He stated that he felt his roof hadn't been nailed properly and wanted us to fix it. Mind you—this is 17 years after he had moved in. I told the customer that I would fix his roof, after all this time, if it was improperly nailed at the time of installation. This was a leap of faith on my part, but I also knew it wouldn't cost that much to satisfy this person.

I sent my Customer Service field manager to investigate and he reported to me what he saw. I contacted an "expert" on the building code to look into what the rules were 17 years ago regarding roof nailing. I also contacted the building department for their input.

This took about three weeks and before I could gather any information, we were served with a subpoena to appear in court. The owner appeared with a folder full of pictures and notes on our conversations, as well as estimates and the actual cost that he paid to do the job. We came with two sheets of paper, one of which was the experts findings and the other from the building department saying that all had passed the code at that time. It's ironic that the same inspector that originally signed off on the roof nailing was still with the department.

The homeowner told the judge that he wasn't upset with The William Lyon Company and actually praised us for our investigation. He just wanted to be reimbursed the $1,400 that it cost him to do his repairs. The judge took this all into consideration and mailed us the results about a week later.

The judge found in our favor and the homeowner could not collect his costs. This isn't the end of the story. About six months later, his daughter bought a new home from us and the reason we were chosen was that her father felt he was treated fairly by the Lyon Company. You just never know where good and honest Customer Service will spread to. This is another example of good Customer Service not costing, but paying.

Customer Service doesn't only apply to the buyer. Every person doing business with the builder is a customer of his in every sense of the word. From the Architect, Engineer, Suppliers and

Subcontractors make up the customer list of the builder. Interest has to be taken in the way they do business and giving help, whenever possible, to keep them in business. Under no circumstances should the relationship of the Master/Slave mentality be allowed to fester. It is in the builders' long term interest that good subcontractors stay alive and thrive.

The very day that the first Iraq war started (1991) I had scheduled a get-together with all our subcontractors at our office board room (we had a huge one). My goal was to explain our Customer Service policies and to find out from them how we could help them have a better business. We had a lot of great subcontractors and they were totally overcome that we had showed that much interest in helping their company to be profitable. It was a great day. We had our expert in Customer Service help overcome any problems that they may be having—either with us or others. Some of the comments afterward were touching. One said that he "couldn't believe that a large builder like The William Company was interested in us making a profit." The answer was quite simple. When you make a profit, so do we.

We had our Customer Service dialed in very tight. Every month we could detect problems occurring on a project before they actually became a problem. One month we noticed a blip on the screen—so to speak—and decided to be pro-active. We called in our representative and discussed with him what it might mean. He wasn't eager to tell or even venture a guess what might be wrong so we decided to have him switch projects with another rep. and see if the blip went away. He was very unhappy about the switch, but we assured him that it had nothing to do with his work, that it just might be a personality adjustment with the owners in that project.

Actually, this rep. did have some problems dealing with people and I'm sure that brought about the blip. He had kind of an attitude defect that made it hard for him to deal with buyers in this buying range. He was much more effective with a lower priced project.

The switch made the blip go away and the rep. that was moved even liked his new project better. Sometimes people are expected to do great things well above their capacity. Challenges are a much needed item, but going too fast or too high might be the wrong move to make. When people are expected to commit to a new philosophy it may take them some time to adjust and some will never adjust.

Another tool I used to get conformance to our new Customer Service policy was to base a part of the superintendent's bonus on the quality of the house he was producing. This wasn't easy since we had a number of old school supers that just hated change. They felt that if they beat the schedule they were owed a bonus. This led to some shoddy work and additional Customer Service headaches that could easily be averted.

I knew that the "inspector" that would make the call on how high up the quality ladder a house went would have to be one that was respected by the supers as being honest and fair. That job could only fit one person and that was my Customer Service field manager. Who else would have a better handle on what the new customer was looking for and had a good rapport with construction.

We also had to have some guidelines so that the supers didn't think we were asking for the moon. Actually what the previous buyers were complaining about became the guidelines for our inspections.

It was amazing how much cooperation we received once the

supers understood that a full one-quarter of there potential bonus was based on this quality inspection. Some complained about the results, but ultimately, the quality of the product improved considerably. We were starting to get very low numbers on our walk-throughs for corrections. In some cases we were getting too many in the zero to five ranges. I suspected a little collusion on the part of the Customer Service rep. and decided to follow up for myself.

This rep. had a walk-through in the morning with zero items and I visited the site in the afternoon. Before I could take two steps in the house I had noticed five things that should have been on the list for corrections. Asked about this, he said that they would have been taken care of before the buyers moved in and so he didn't put them down. This defeated the entire process. We needed to know what was really happening in the field and not reading some padded information. This didn't happen again.

We also set up an award system based on the previous quarters work. This was for the best superintendent, assistant superintendent and customer service rep. based on all the numbers we would accumulate as well as their supervisor's recommendations. Sometimes this was very hard since many had risen to the top of their profession. A few times feelings got hurt when a person thought they should have won instead of the other guy. Although this did happen, it actually inspired those that lost to do better the next quarter. This would only happen if they really felt that the judging was being done fairly.

The awards were monetary and very welcome by the winners. As the years rolled on and the construction industry was taking the 1992 plunge it became apparent that spending had to be reined in. My idea was to use US Saving Bonds since we could actually give away the same amount of money, but it would only cost us one-half. This worked for several quarters and as the economic situation worsened this also was disposed of. It was amazing that some of the comments, when we made the first cutback, were of how cheap we were getting. Most had never had a US Savings Bond before and didn't quite know what to make of it.

Several months later, the boom came down and the company, as we knew it, was entirely changed. The famous St. Valentines Day massacre in Chicago had nothing over this event. Divisions as well as a great number of personnel were dismissed unceremoniously, including me. The banks were now in charge. It had nothing to do with the General's ability to run his company, but rather the banks had a great deal of money invested and wanted a front row seat to direct the action.

Now the customer's name would fall out of the rolodex one minute after the one year warranty was up. The banks were not willing to spend one nickel after the warranty period. The General was still anxious about his customers. He hired my Customer Service manager to visit everyone that complained to evaluate the problem. If it was the fault of the company, he would pay it out of his own pocket. The banks didn't have much to say about what came out of his pocket. General Lyon has since rebounded to, again, be a major player in the building industry. His word was as good as gold even when astronomical circumstances, beyond his control, crippled his company for a number of years. I am living proof of that.

ARE YOU BEING SERVED YET?: CUSTOMER SERVICE EVOLUTION

News story—Cyndy Legowski in center; author on right

*The William Lyon Co. awards luncheon—
Cyndy Legowski on the left; author on the right*

*The William Lyon Co. awards Luncheon—
Dave Coughlin standing; Cyndy Legowski next to tree*

ARE YOU BEING SERVED YET?: CUSTOMER SERVICE EVOLUTION

My first day at new Lyon office

My new office in my "died and went to heaven job"

The Next Best—

The most prolonged employment period I had in my 41 years in the industry was with The Konwiser Corporation, also of Newport Beach, CA. During my eleven and one-half years I went from a Superintendent to General Superintendent to Field Operations Manager. We built apartments, condominiums and a few single family homes. We also had a number of special projects of which one was the first co-generation plant for apartments west of the Mississippi. The boss always said that he wouldn't experiment and let some other builder plow the new ground first. During my stay, he got us involved in many new projects that other builders wouldn't touch. This just made things different and exciting.

Our best attempt at Customer Service came when we had about 2300 apartments to maintain.

For years, Customer Service was of minimal quality with minimal personnel. There was a feeling that if the renter didn't like the apartment, they could move out. This also caused a problem, since the condition it was brought back to; to rent again, was well below par. This condition caused many units to stay vacant for a long period of time.

The company policy was that the managers were the ones to get the units ready to rent. It was also a policy that this was only to take three days. First of all, all the managers were women and many had no idea which ends of the paint brush to grab. The second problem was that what they thought was a completed unit was not what a new renter thought. Thus, the average vacancy period was 29-1/2 days. This equated to approximately a half-million dollars in potential rents that were missed out on and it wasn't getting any better.

The boss was getting really upset with the managers and they were getting more and more frustrated that they started to "fib" about the readiness of the units. I was asked to visit several projects to check on their readiness. As it turned out, none were ready for move-in and most had several days' worth of work yet to do to make them ready. Plus being late in delivering a ready unit, the quality of the repairs was terrible. You just can't expect people, whose job it is to rent the units to also be top notch repair people. Something had to be done, and fast.

I devised a program that would radically change the way units were being repaired. We first looked at all the problems and then listed possibilities to overcome these deficiencies. One example was that with about 23 different managers there were the bossy ones and the quite ones. The bossy ones were able to badger the painters and carpet cleaners to come to their place first. This would send chaos throughout the company and the others would complain that they couldn't get service. They were always asking for different painters.

Another problem we had to overcome was that 23 different managers had 23 different ideas as to how to complete a unit and what was acceptable. How would we overcome this fractured way of doing business? One thing was for sure, we could not let it go on any longer.

We needed one person to schedule everything and one person to verify what was being done. Then we needed to talk with the subcontractors that were to be involved and agree to price as well as the appropriate procedures they needed to take to make it all work. About two weeks later we gave it a try.

The two people I picked were absolutely the best we could have ever asked for. They were, without a doubt, perfectly matched to their positions. The scheduler (Gilda Stern) and the inspector (Sammy Davis) brought both positions to the ultimate efficiency level and the average down days per unit shrank to five and seven days (normal or trashed unit). This cut the vacancy time down by 75 percent and brought the quality level up many notches.

We already had between five and seven Customer Service people on board at this time so we worked out a better schedule where "teams" would tackle various projects, per schedule, so that the five and seven day time period could be maintained. Several Customer Service personnel would be assigned to outside maintenance and several others to the inside. Therefore, the every day type maintenance problems were covered as well as the scheduled turn-over rate of the unoccupied units.

We had our own warehouse of replacement parts and bought them in quantity at wholesale prices. We very seldom had to wait for parts. We also had our own specialists in the group which could do electrical, plumbing, drywall, stucco and carpentry repairs. This saved many dollars as well as kept things on schedule.

The landscaping was a pet peeve with the boss. He would walk the projects at least every month and give the landscape maintenance people a long list of items to correct. This really got to be a hassle, since we had numerous companies doing the landscape work on all our far flung projects. There was no way that these people would do everything the boss wanted and that even upset him more.

It got to the point that the frustration grew too great and I was asked to do something about it. I contacted the original installer of the landscaping as this person did every project we built and asked him to look at the maintenance angle. First he didn't want to do all the projects, but it wasn't too hard to talk him into it. This was a company that the boss had the utmost confidence in and was thankful that it was finally agreed to service the maintenance end. This landscape company knew about Customer Service. They would bend over backwards to please and they made money doing it.

Every year the time came to raise the rents. This letter usually set off many to hand in their moving notice. We had quite a few give their notice, go out looking for another place to rent and then come back in and withdraw their notice. Their reason was that although they could find cheaper rents, they couldn't find a better maintained complex with great Customer Service. You just never know how great Customer Service will pay off, but it definitely will.

Customer service comes in many different forms. The kind that we are most familiar with is where you call a company and complain about something. The other kind is where you, or your company, do something that benefits any number of people without the expectation of being reimbursed. We did a number of the latter while I was with The Konwiser Corp. The owner was quite philanthropic and many times he would come to me and tell me what had to be done and let me figure out how it could be done.

During this period, he and his wife were officers in a group that helped out single, battered wives and mothers. It was a great group and they had large plans to help their cause. One of these plans was to provide cubicles or booths for the well-known interior decorators, in this well-to-do area, to show off their skills.

The plan was to provide eight by eight foot areas for them to decorate anyway they wanted to and allow the public to view their creations—for a price. This all happened during the end of the year and the idea of decorating one's home was on many people's minds.

The group had one of the finest hotels in the area donate their large meeting room for this gathering. It would also be good for the hotel to get people into their establishment and see how fine it really was.

We were told how many booths we would need—which were around 30+ and how much time we would have in completing this construction. Generally the requirements were; couldn't start before 6:00 PM and had to be finished before 2:00 AM the following morning.

We planned all the material and had it delivered to the hotel. It was dropped in back where all deliveries were made and had to be carried in by hand. We also had to mark out the floor with tape because all this building was over their very expensive carpet and we couldn't damage it in any way.

These were to be all free standing and only leaning on each other for support. Everything was going fine until about 9:00 PM when some of the decorators started to show up. This caused a lot of confusion since they were starting to throw all their things around and telling us how they wanted their specific booth.

This was not the agreement, but we suffered through and came up with a plan to speed things up so we could get out of there quicker. Just being surrounded and outnumbered by all those interior decorators was very intimidating. We "macho" construction people were definitely in the wrong room and escape was the only thing on our minds. We finished up around midnight and turned the whole thing over to them. I understand that the show was a great success and it was decided that the next year they would do the same thing.

The next year I was lucky and got sick on the way to the hotel. My son was following me and I waved him over—after I expelled everything I ate that day—and told him to take over and I was returning home. I also understand that this one was also a success, but it wasn't repeated the following year.

We also were involved with school remodeling. This came about at the private school that the owner's son was attending. Apparently the school needed some work done and all of a sudden the entire company was involved.

I was also involved in building an addition to the bosses' house. This wasn't just an ordinary addition, but rather it was like putting five pounds of "stuff" into a three pound bag. There was no way of getting to their back yard—the conventional way, but the need of an eighty ton crane was the tool of choice. Their back yard was about ten feet below their house and the street in the rear was about twenty-five feet below that. All the material needed to lifted up and stored on this postage size lot for a train room that was dug into their rear bank.

This meant that even the "cat" that was needed to dig out the foundation needed to be lifted up on the lot. It also needed room to operate and then we also had to get rid of the dirt. We made a dirt slide which ended up in a dump truck and eventually it was completely dug out. Then down came the "cat."

When it was all finished, it looked great. You could hardly see the actual building because it was dug in the bank so far. It also had a dirt roof which had a train locomotive design in the planting. The total train room was finished sometime later and probably enjoyed more as a conversation piece than a hobby room.

These last few examples really show that a person with the ability to dream, willing to experiment and think ahead is also the kind of person that is needed in customer service. To remain stagnant or be unwilling to experiment or plan ahead cannot possible plan great customer service. It takes a person with imagination and the willingness to try something new to be able to satisfy customer's needs.

All the time, while you are doing this, you cannot forget to maintain the high values and principles that customer service stands for. You cannot just throw something at the customer and hope it works, but rather plan new things that you're quite sure the customer would like.

Konwiser Corp. picnic with Mr. Konwiser at right

Company had a surprise birthday party for Mr. Konwiser, at right

BBQ for customer service staff at author's house

ARE YOU BEING SERVED YET?: CUSTOMER SERVICE EVOLUTION

Mr. Konwiser as a chauffeur at my daughter's wedding. He did the same for my other daughter a year later.

The Worst—

The company, that I shall call the S·R Company, was, without a doubt, the worst at Customer Service. Even though I was the Director of Customer Service, the construction was so bad that you just couldn't make it right with the customer. I don't mean that the buildings were in danger of falling down, but the small little things were overlooked and they caused giant problems later on. The reason I don't mention their name is that they are doing much better today. They have new personnel in the construction end and the units just have to come out better.

The supervisors spent most of their time in their office making all sorts of reports that were needed for one meeting or another and not much time was spent on supervision of the project. They would look out the door to see if certain subcontractors showed up and then mark it down on the schedule. They always seemed to be on schedule, but way behind on the quality.

This was a condominium project with eight separate buildings, all with a different number of units in each. All were three story buildings with an elevator and parking underneath. Not easy buildings to build, especially in the hilly part of a Northern California city.

The first building was completed and as the first buyers moved in, deficiencies started to appear. Some of these were considered "normal" Customer Service stuff and some had to do with construction irregularities that were promised to be corrected on the next building. As the first building came on line in the fall, we didn't have long to wait until the rains started. The first rains opened Pandora's Box and it was never closed.

Construction put band-aid after band-aid on the problems and finally the rains stopped and they declared a victory. The buyers settled down, a little, and progress was made on the second building.

As so often happens, the rains came again in the fall and low and behold, the same problem not only happened on the second building, except worse, but it also happened again on the first building. In the very same spots that were "fixed" the previous year. Construction just couldn't figure it out. They really got serious this time and threatened all the subs to get the leaks fixed. Well—they couldn't since some of the subs were from hundreds of miles away and just couldn't send a crew to do repairs. This is one of the prices that had to be paid if you wanted the bottom dollar on the bid.

Construction then took it upon themselves, again, to fix the problems. They went through the motions both inside and out and after awhile, the rains stopped. Again they declared victory and they continued to build buildings 3 and 4.

I don't have to tell you what happened the next time it rained. Now they had four buildings that were major leakers. Not only didn't they fix the previous problems, but the new buildings were getting worse.

We didn't have many other problems that upset the buyers nearly as much as these leaks. We were able to keep control of everything except the leaks. I continually complained to my superior that construction has to build them better, since Customer Service couldn't do it after the buyer moved in.

There was quite the discussion with construction and my superior returned and said that it would be MY PROBLEM and I had to fix it, because construction wouldn't. I was expected to make sure the lath and plaster went on properly so there wouldn't be any leaks because construction couldn't do it. I informed them that I knew what was wrong, but I had neither the personnel nor budget to manage this part of construction.

This all fell on deaf ears and the stress was mounting. When I finally realized that they wanted me to be part of the problem and not part of the solution, I resigned my position. This action on my part did start a change in the company. Several months later my superior was canned. Then several months after that the head of construction, who had become a fixture, was dispensed with. My Customer Service representative on the project bailed out right after me, because he realized also that he would become the fall guy.

This problem continued throughout the eight buildings, and by some reports even got worse. I feel sorry for those buyers that had the problem because it really was a great location with a great view. I know that all of the 433 buyers did not have these problems, but being in a homeowner's association, they really are part of it.

If this was the only project that all these problems occurred, you could blame the design or site personnel for some of these abominations. But we had a number of other projects that were new as well as older ones being converted to condominiums. Many of these same problems occurred in nearly every project.

The main problem is that cutting corners in the bidding process cost many times more in obtaining the satisfaction of the customer. It proves the point that you can have great Customer Service, but if the product is bad, you just can't do enough to redeem yourself.

For years afterward, the history and reputation of this project was known throughout the state and I always had to explain that I bailed out before I got run over. The company eventually put some great construction people in charge and I'm sure this sad chapter is just a memory. What hurts the most is that a reputation was ruined so quickly and it takes so long to build it back up again. I hope they are past this part forever.

Next to Worst—

I've forgotten the name of this builder, but the memory of working with him will stay with me for a long time. There wasn't anything really bad about this builder, except that he was deathly afraid to talk with his buyers.

I started with this builder when I was in charge of *Home Team*, which was a Customer Service supplement for the builder. *Home Team* was the answer to many builders who didn't want to be involved with Customer Service.

We met on a Friday afternoon and were told that the walk-throughs would begin on Tuesday. I asked him what week and he said next week. Looking at the homes in question, I said that it would take a week of hard work to get them ready. He said his supt. was special and had things all planned out and Tuesday was the day.

Tuesday came and the progress didn't look that much advanced from the time I saw it before. Walking a house with a buyer, over trash and boxes, dirt on the counters, the appliances not installed and wet paint all over was not my idea of being in move-in condition. Even the buyers wondered why we were doing it when it was obviously not ready to move in. The list was a mile long and the builder looked surprised. It was quite obvious that he hadn't looked at the house before.

Nearly every house was in the same condition as the first one. This was a case of trying to close an escrow two weeks before completion. The buyers all became quite angry and a few refused to close. Some had to move in, because they didn't have any other place to go. It was a bad start for this builder, because the houses themselves were well designed.

As the Customer Service end of this builder, we had the insurmountable task of trying to keep the customers happy. I suggested to the builder that since they all had their walk-through before the house was complete that they should have another walk-through now that it was. The builder wasn't too keen on this idea. He thought this might open a Pandora's Box scenario or they might now find many other things that needed to be corrected. Here again, the thought of money coming out of his pocket was uppermost in his mind.

I continually suggested that he would be in more trouble if we didn't schedule another walk-through. Of course I wasn't going to do this for free, but considering what costs law suits would bring him, he really didn't have much choice. We scheduled about three to four a day and they all were received with surprise and thankfulness. We made sure that what we couldn't cover on the original walk was covered on this one.

Everyone went well. The buyers were delighted that they had a second chance and they didn't seem to take unfair advantage of it. Most of the items could never have been checked out on the first walk. One owner had already threatened the builder with a law suit over a problem with the grading. He mentioned that all he wanted was for the builder to come out and look at the problem. He said that was his only real problem. I mentioned to him that I would be speaking with the builder shortly and would mention this to him again.

I hadn't told the buyer that the builder was only two houses away. It seemed to me that it would be a perfect time for the builder to overcome an unhappy customer and avoid a possible law suit. The builder was surprised that the buyer wanted him to just look at the problem and said that the next day he would try and get by. I suggested that positive results could be achieved in the next 15 minutes and all he had to do was walk 200 feet and ring the bell. He said, "Maybe I'll do that." I needed to be on the project for another hour or so, but the builder never made it. What a blunder. A problem could have been solved, a reputation saved and a law suit avoided just by ringing the bell.

Home Team—

Home Team was an idea that was developed to help the builder through their worst part of building a house—the buyer move-in. The builder wants the buyer to move in, but really wants them to close their escrow, whether they move in or not. That is the pay-off for the builder. Once the buyer moves in, it generally signifies that some of that money the builder just made might have to be spent to do some repairs. It's like reaching in his pocket and stealing his money.

Being of any size at all, a builder should have a person or persons that are customer oriented to handle any correction matters. Generally though, they make their superintendent or his assistant confront the buyer and attempt the corrections. First of all, neither the superintendent nor his assistants want anything to do with the buyer. Secondly, this attitude generally leaves a bad taste in the buyer's mouth. They feel they are getting the short end of the stick and the run-around. Basically, this is really what happens.

Now to have professionals take over that duty was a god-send to the supers. They were anxious to unload their homes on to somebody else's responsibility. Guidelines needed to be implemented so that we wouldn't be saddled with work that really belonged to the builder and his crew. We offered additional help in the form of service personnel, at additional cost, to lend a hand with the multitude of final details needed for a house to become a home. Many took us up on this idea and their walks went much smoother and the customers were much happier.

We were also called upon to investigate problems that occurred in homes well past the warranty period. One builder had us investigate a house that was settling with numerous cracks. Another, why some expensive marble, used as a backsplash in the kitchen, was turning colors. Both were fairly easy to detect, but the builder wanted us to do it so they wouldn't have to go there in person.

Home Team tried to offer everything we could think of to make the move-in process more enlightening to the new homeowner. We developed a new homeowner seminar, to be held several weeks prior to actual move-in, to show how the houses were built and what to expect upon move-in. Of course we had to charge for this, but the benefits were well worth it. The builder was skeptical and we had to talk long and hard for him to see the value.

These seminars were only about two hours long and would be held on a Saturday morning in one of their model garages. I had a slide presentation and then we would answer any of their questions. We had donuts and coffee and the buyers got to meet their neighbors prior to actually moving in. They enjoyed the get-together and it went a long way for making the walk-through and the move-in experience much easier.

Home Team was a great idea and served many builders well. However, many builders took advantage of our services and failed to really complete the homes for their buyers. They figured that we should actually do the final touches, such as; hang light fixtures, set appliances, pick up trash and clean. The superintendents of these builders were only too happy to stop their responsibility about 95% through.

Construction and Customer Service are like oil and water. One deals with the macho side of life and the other with the real world. Construction personnel almost have a passion about not getting involved with the buyer. It's like the buyer has some sort of contagious disease or something. Again, we haven't come very far in Customer Service since I first got into the business.

As *Home Team* grew, the builders realized that they really needed to finish their homes and *Home Team* was only hired to take care of complaints that may arise in the one year warranty period. Since most builders really hate Customer Service they still were afraid to turn their customers over to a third party. We would have weekly meetings with all sorts of data to keep the builder fully informed. We had to continually prove ourselves every week. You would have thought that the builder was the expert on Customer Service.

Every time something went wrong, Home Team would have their feet put to the fire. We would be questioned and critiqued beyond belief. We felt like wooden ducks in a shooting gallery. It was amazing how critical the builder could get with us, but overlooking their own faults. Kind of like the splinter in your neighbor's eye while you have a log in you own. The builder wanted the very best from Home Team while willing to only pay for mediocrity. If all their Customer Service had been left up to the builder, the problems would have ended up in court for sure. Builders only know one thing and that is the building end of construction. Actually, they don't know that very well either. Their best suit is financing and deal making. Customer Service really never enters the picture in most builders' minds. This is quite evident when you look at their budgets. Customer Service is usually the last item on the list with very little money applied.

One builder had applied $500 for each unit to handle Customer Service. This was also to cover the wages of the CS Rep. who was to do the work. The final accounting was well over $1,500 per unit, not counting the reps. wages. They would not accept the fact that the overages could be attributed directly back to the bad construction practices and not irresponsible Customer Service procedures.

Will builders ever change? Probably not on their own. The only builder that changed in my 41 years in the industry was General Lyon of The William Lyon Company. He was the leading instrument in changing the entire company from an average builder to a giant among giants. Only he could have made it work. Only the very top personnel can start and maintain great Customer Service. The program is doomed to failure if not initiated by the very top.

How does the builder start to change? He listens to his customers. The buyers of his product will tell him how he is doing and what he should do to be better. However, a smart builder will have first hand knowledge of this before he hears it from his buyers. You have to be pro-active in the building business or the competition will pass you up.

A builder also listens to his other customers—his suppliers and subcontractors. Many are able to offer new and different ways of doing business as well as introduce new and/or better products to make the builder's houses a leader. The builder needs to invest in these customers just like he would in a normal business partnership. It is very important for the builder that his subcontractors and suppliers succeed in business.

The William Lyon Company knew how to do this—at least The Central Counties Division did. We maintained a list of qualified subcontractors and for a new entry to make it on the list was really hard. Not only did they have to pass the normal requirements, but needed to have real value in their work. This meant they also needed a good Customer Service department of their own.

One subcontractor was dropped from the list because of their Customer Service office manager. Their field employees were great, but we received many complaints from our homeowners due to the rudeness of the manager. When the subcontractor was told of this discrepancy they had to really review where their company was heading. Their Customer Service manager was the owner's daughter. They did do something about it and six months later they called to say that problem had been eliminated and they would like to get back on the list. They hadn't realized how important Customer Service was until it was responsible for them losing new work.

Home Team would indoctrinate the new homeowner in how a new home operates and what needs to be done to keep it running. So many new homeowners were so excited about their new purchase that they had trouble concentrating on the indoctrination. Many would bring their children and let them run all over the house. It was very hard to concentrate with disturbances like that.

We also published homeowner manuals for some of the builders. This information was strictly tailored to their project and homes and contained nearly everything a new buyer needs to know. However, the effort was wasted on many new buyers. They would throw the manual in the closet and then call or write us to complain that something was wrong. Many times we would refer them to a specific section in the manual that would answer their question and they would sheepishly admit that they didn't read it and actually couldn't remember where they placed it.

Home Team was one of the brightest ideas to come along in many years. It was absolutely the right thing for the right time. I couldn't stop exhorting the benefits of *Home Team*. It was the culmination of all that I wanted to see in customer service. It definitely was an answer to a builder's problem of being afraid of the customer. However, the marketing of *Home Team* was not thought out well enough. The owner and the company that was putting together the promotion always seemed to be at odds with each other. It really had to do with the amount of money that this program was costing.

We would have meeting after meeting and usually wound up talking money. They developed all sorts of stuff for us, but somehow missed the main ingredient—the builder. The builder was impressed with all the colors and flyers, but the program didn't grab their wallet and make them sign-up. Some came close, but that only counts in hand grenades and horseshoes.

Since we could see the dire need for this service, the thought was that the builder could also see the need.

After finding our way for a year or so, a group in Northern California developed a similar operation. This wasn't the first group to do so, but it was the best financed group by far.

We had several accounts in the "Bay" area and all of a sudden we were competing against a new comer. We didn't mind, but later found out that the playing field wasn't quite level.

A friend of mine worked for them, but I didn't know that until I started to look her up one day. I hadn't heard from her in some time and thought it would be nice to see her again. I had originally got her and the company she worked for then to sell and install the flooring in the 433 condominium project in Oakland. The next thing I know is that she was working for this customer service outfit.

I was able to contact her and heard all about the great things they were doing and how sophisticated their operation was. In fact, she sent me an airline ticket to come visit them. I was always curious how others were doing this kind of work and gladly accepted.

I have to admit, they had a large and well supplied operation. They had vehicles, radios, uniforms, computers and all the necessary items to really carry off their program. I was dazzled! Especially when I looked at our operation and realized that I was the only one (at that time) in ours and used my own vehicle.

Several months later we lost a job to them because they had a laptop computer and it had a PowerPoint program to show the customer. They also had the advantage to making deals on the golf course.

About a month later, one of the principals arrived at our office in Southern California to pay a visit. He didn't say at the time, but I knew that they were looking to open an office in the area and meet us head-on.

This was about the time when we changed offices and could only keep tabs on them through word of mouth. Soon word came back that my "friend" was no longer with them and I never heard from her again. I did hear, however, that they began a slide backwards due to very strange business practices. I was happy to hear that that what was rumored, finally came to light. I hate to see businesses go bad, but when they are not playing fair to start with, they deserve their fate.

I don't believe the builder has changed in the last forty years or so. They want all contact with the customer to stop the instant the escrow papers are signed. That is why there are so many law suits involving builders. The customer feels cheated almost as soon as they move in. All the promises that the sales department gave them didn't seem to be transferred to the builder and now the friction starts.

The 3 P's of Customer Service—

Once you sift out all the normal problems that a builder/developer encounter, such as money, land, etc., I believe there are only (3) major categories that a company needs to really concern themselves with. They are:

Product
Performance
Personnel

To answer the questions that were asked of me in a memo from management, regarding what hampers personnel from implementing the basic principles of fair play and customer awareness and what can we do to improve or change it, is not easily answered in just a few words. If I may indulge you for a few minutes of reading, I would like to have you visualize the larger picture. I need to tie these three items together before the inevitable outcome becomes apparent.

PRODUCT: Whether new, used or conversions, the product is the only substance for which the reputation of a company can be built. The quality has to be built in and cannot be added on. This doesn't mean that it has to be expensive. It just has to be the best it can be in the class that it will sell in. Every dollar that is saved initially and fails to perform in the long run will cost four dollars to fix. Those that are into converting and selling units that were originally rented will find the original product selection and the quality of that selection to be a hindrance with the customer. Most buyers today will recognize the difference between a Chevrolet or Buick compared to a Pinto or a Yugo. There are generally so many good things going for most units that it is a shame that the want of a decent faucet could overshadow a great view or a great layout.

I believe that much more time is spent making sure the subcontractor is on the job instead of making sure the performance of the subcontractor is up to par. Some of the faults that have been found in many projects had more to do with oversight, lack of experience or flagrant disregard of proper construction practices by the subcontractor. This usually comes when the selection of the subcontractor is done by price alone. I am quite sure if the superintendent had the time to inspect all aspects of the building, most of these problems would never show up.

Subcontractors need to be brought into the group as "partners" in a project. They need to know that the very survival of the project is in their hands. The need to commit to providing the very best they can for the most reasonable price. And, in return, you need to make sure they can count on your company to pay them on time for their efforts.

This partnership will increase the quality many times over. They will be more excited to come to work and do a good job. They will be more responsive to correcting any faults that are found. They will perform their Customer Service duties with a true feeling that they were sorry that their product didn't hold up better. The builder's after construction costs will go down dramatically. The more often quality is practiced in the beginning the less you have to sell quality in the end.

PERFORMANCE: This is how the customer sees us and not how fast you can build them. The higher the performance in this area the less cost to the company and the larger the profits will be. Selling the product honestly, trying to understand what the customer wants and doing your best to deliver is the only way that customer will pass your name along to their friends as a great place to shop. Anything less will get either no response, because the person feels cheated and embarrassed, or a very verbal one which will keep customers away in droves.

Since our subcontractors are also our customers, what better way to advertise? If one subcontractor bought a unit, wouldn't that say something to the buying public? If they buy one, they must be good. After all, they helped build it and they know how it's built. This approach needs only to sell one or two units in the entire project to overcome any extra that was spent to get the quality. You just have to ask any subcontractor, which project would they buy in and you will know where you stand. Some potential buyers will even ask people in the industry to how a certain builder operates. This alone can make or break many sales.

PERSONNEL: The back bone of any business is the personnel that carry the company image to the public every day. Personnel need to feel wanted and needed. The need to know that everything they do directly reflects on the reputation of the company. They also need to feel that the great things they do are recognized by the company and rewarded in some form.

Recognizing an individual or group is the highest form of reward. A person needs to feel that the company is taking care of their basics automatically. When they feel this is accomplished they will perform at their highest level possible with just a pat on the back or some tangible evidence of their accomplishments. Others will work harder to reach the same or higher goals just so they won't feel left out. Nothing inspires a person to do their best than the thought that they will be recognized in a fair and meaningful way.

This team work or pride in their accomplishments can save many times the money it would cost. The projects come out better, the level of quality is higher, customers feel that there is something different about this project. When personnel seem committed to doing a good job, the customer is much less anxious about something going wrong or wondering if it would be fixed—if it did go wrong.

The customer will remember the service long after the price. They may have bought for the price, but wont buy again or promote the product to friends if the service is not right. In order for the service to be right, the quality has to be built in and the personnel need to feel good about their work.

The 3—P's need to be worked on all together. Any one or two without the other(s) will only give short lived results. You cannot have a great product if quality and excited and concerned personnel are not involved. Without these the customer is, possibly, a one timer. You can't sustain a business with the customer being treated as an expendable.

I believe that every business needs to reinvent their wheel and really take stock of their mission statement.

Several sayings that come to mind are very appropriate at this point...

"If you always do, what you always did, you will always get what you always got"

The 1970 saying that *"if it ain't broken, don't fix it,"* has changed into the 2000 version, *"if it works, it's obsolete."*

How to be successful in the new millennium is to *"exceed people's expectations...Including your own."*

*Sayings from
Tom Callister's Resource Management and Marketing Solutions*

I presented this in response to a memo from management only to be rebuffed. I really had violated a cardinal rule about telling the higher ups how their business should be run. It seemed strange though, they asked and I told them. Needless to say not much happened and soon the entire construction department was doing it their way again.

It wasn't long after I left that the light started to shine through and major changes did take place. This is a prime example of company politics outweighing common sense. Those that had been there for some time and had gained favor with the powers-that-be were still able to sway the company's direction. It was only after overwhelming evidence accumulated and the legal bills were starting to pile up that the principals were anxious to act. I'm sure they felt like they were discovering these ongoing problems for the first time and forgot about the warnings received earlier.

This memo could be applied to almost any company in the building business today. We have not progressed very far over the last half century. Customer Service is still a problem that few companies want to face and overcome. And, we, the customer or consumer, are largely at fault.

I think we complain more now that in the past, but unless we're willing to carry it to the limit, such as a law suit, we would rather kick the builder or company out of your life, badmouth them if you get a chance and live with the frustration. Actually you tend to dismiss bad service as not having time for this "crap" in your life. Like "who needs it?" What this really does is dismiss the problem in the company's eyes and let them off the hook to do it all over again. Customers/consumers need to have stamina and see the problem through.

Keeping your problem in front of those you ask to fix it will pay off in the end. You may feel like you're talking to the wall, but believe me; your message is getting through. When I was in construction usually those that had a squeaky wheel got the oil.

Some companies go way overboard on Customer Service. I do not advocate that practice either. It always seems like the pendulum never stays in the middle, but rather far to one side or the other. Take for instance, Nordstrom Department Stores. They are known for their outstanding Customer Service—or they were. A story was floating around that a sales person took back a set of automobile tires for credit when Nordstrom doesn't even sell tires. To me this is plain stupid. If you don't sell it, you can't take it back for credit—period.

Of course, there are many other stories that speak well for their operation. I have to admit that it has been some time since I've been in one of their stores. But, I do remember the last time and the experience was memorable. Now if they would only lower their prices a little...

I think you can see that overdoing Customer Service will cause problems as well. Normal people would not take tires back to Nordstrom's and ask for credit. But, they would expect service on items that they do sell. If you give people the service they expect, you are way ahead of the game. If the customer receives more than they expect, they could be a customer for life.

Signs of Bad Customer Service—

"They're all like that."
"We can't change it."
"We only warrant that item for ninety days."
"Without the receipt we can't do anything."
"That's just the nature of the product."
"What do you expect for only $ - - - - -?"
"We don't sell that product anymore."

I'm sure all of you have heard at least one of these in your lifetime. Nothing will sour you on patronizing an establishment more than to be told that it's your problem and not theirs.

When a builder's Customer Service person answers your request and tells you that "all of the other houses are the same way" call him on it. I had a neighbor ask me once if I had holes under my kitchen sink. I told him no, why? Well, he has and the service person said that all the houses had holes under the sink and didn't patch them.

This service person was from a temporary agency helping out and I know that she would never have said that if she hadn't been instructed to by the regular service person. You heard me right—she. This young woman is the same one that I had hired a number of years before to do Customer Service for me. She was the kind to overdo things and not find ways to say no. I told my neighbor to send in another service request and state that you didn't care if every house had holes under the sink, you want yours fixed.

I had some shrubs on my bank at the rear of my house and eight of them turned brown. Out of the thirty five plus shrubs, eight died. They weren't just in one area so the watering pattern might not be the culprit, but rather located with others of the same kind throughout the bank area. First I was told that I hadn't watered them properly. Then he saw that others right next to the dead ones were alive and well. Then I was told that the landscaper only warrants his plants for 90 days. When I told him the Home Depot and Lowe's warrant all their plants for a year, he changed his tune again. Then he said that he would try and talk the landscaper into some new ones, but couldn't promise anything. Several weeks later, eight new shrubs showed up, but they wouldn't dig out the dead ones and plant the new ones. I didn't want them to do that either since I watched how they planted the shrubs originally and it's a miracle that any of them lived. By the way—all eight plants are thriving!

One of the most reported items on a new home is the cracks in the stucco. The industry standard is really hard for the customer to fathom. If you can stick a dime in a crack, it should be fixed. Many builders change the dime to a quarter and some would like to change it to a roll of quarters. This fault is nearly impossible to keep from happening. However, if more attention was paid to the mixture of sand, cement and water, the problem would be much less. For years the mixture has been getting to be much more sand than the industry standard. Unless you count every shovel full of sand that goes in the mixture, you'll never know if you are being cheated or not. Sand costs much less than cement.

Another much reported correction is on the painting. The builder gives you a touch-up kit so you can take care of any flaws in the painting. However, if you don't look at the painting carefully before you accept the house, you will need a lot more paint than comes in the kit.

My biggest complaint in my last new home was the landscaping. Just watching some of the workers, you just know that it would be a cold day in hell before all the plants started to grow. I had asked for a landscape plan that they followed. They provided one—for the wrong tract. Then they faxed me another and it had lots of stuff on it that wasn't on my lot. Their office seemed so surprised that they sent out a supervisor to look it over. He couldn't figure it out either. The plan and what was planted differed wildly. They corrected this error in the next day or two. However, the plan for the bank was to have another type of groundcover also, but was not planted. They took care of that omission as well. But, then six months later, they came back and planted it again. They had forgotten about the first planting. Kind of funny, if you weren't paying them. But can you imagine how a company can stay in business when screw ups like this occur almost every day?

Another example of bad service was when a service rep. came to do some repainting on the second floor of a woman's house. This service rep. wasn't very careful and was normally referred to as the bull in a china shop. Every time he had painting to do he always carried in a five gallon can of paint. No drop cloth. This owner owned a small dog and told the service rep. she had to go to the store and would take her dog with her. That seemed like a good idea to the rep. as he continued to paint. As luck would have it, just before the woman returned, he backed up and knocked over the paint all over the carpet. When she arrived back, the dog immediately ran upstairs and started barking. The rep. grabbed the dog, rolled it around in the paint, and then hollered down to the owner to get her dog—he just tipped over my paint!

This same Customer Service Rep. is credited with many stories such as this one. How he was allowed to go as far as he did, is beyond me. Some of the stories would be really hard to imagine, but I can assure you that they are more fact than fiction.

Asked to patch a hole in the patio, where a temporary power pole had been located, this service rep. immediately saw a hole near the front porch and assumed this must be the one in question. He mixed up some cement and poured it into the hole and left the job. A day later the owner called to say that his sewer had backed up and wanted us to clear it. We took one look at the hole and realized that he had poured cement down a sewer cleanout. This service rep. was a person that had been in the building business for a long time and had a license to be in business for himself. The patio hole was still there. Needless to say, it caused a big problem plus costing lots of money to repair.

Every now and again, the Customer Service work would slow down and the boss would have this rep. do odd jobs just to stay busy. One such time, he was told to paint the patio fences brown at an apartment complex that was owned by the company. I arrived about an hour after he started to find that all the shrubs in front of these fences were also painted brown. You really couldn't tell where the bushes stopped and the fence began. I asked him why he didn't use a drop cloth to cover the shrubs and he said the he didn't have the time to do it. He was afraid that if he didn't finish that day, he would catch heck from his boss. He didn't stop to think how much trouble he would be in when the boss saw all the shrubs painted brown.

Another one of these open times the boss asked him to come to the office to paint some new cabinets he just had installed. The remodeling of the office was fairly extensive and the new carpet and Formica tops were really bright colors as well as quite expensive. This service rep. started to work with his spray gun and a two foot by two foot tarp (which was just big enough to handle the paint and the compressor). It took him about thirty minutes to complete the job and then he picked up his material and equipment only to find that under his tarp was the only unpainted spot in the office. The boss nearly had a heart attack. Red checked carpet and red countertops all had a heavy misting of white paint. He never thought that spraying would paint anything besides what he aimed at.

I must bring up one more story out of the many to choose from. This rep. wasn't a bad person and, in fact, he was quite likable. He would do almost anything for you. He was always willing to help (although you didn't always want his help).

We sold a condominium to a couple that wanted another door installed. It was still in the construction stage and wasn't too much bother. This service rep. was asked to install the new door. He came by to see what was needed. I told him the size and where it was to be located. But instead of buying a new door frame, he decided to save the boss some money and make his own. He went over to where the rough carpenters were working and came back with some rough sawn 1" x 6" which would be used for roof sheeting.

I visited him once a day—for three days—as he was trying to

make this rough lumber look like a finished door jamb. I finally called the boss and told him that three days at this project was totally wasted since the almost finished product looked like a three year old had been playing in drywall mud. The rep. was using drywall mud to "mould" a door jamb over the 1" x 6" rough lumber. I had asked him why he didn't just buy a door jamb and he said that the boss would get all over him for spending money.

The buyer had come by on the third day and immediately called the office to say that if that was any indication of the finish work, he would cancel the sale. So the buyer and the boss met at the condominium that night and even the boss had to hang his head.

The service rep. really felt bad. He thought he was doing the right thing. He even missed his uncle's funeral because he wanted to finish this job. He was totally dedicated to this company—it was just that he had trouble doing some things right.

Most people do not get to see many of these problems. However, the companies that this kind of service rep. works for do. How they correct it or deal with it will tell how embedded Customer Service is to their operation. This service rep. was eventually let go and stories of this magnitude soon ended. Businesses that want to stay in business can not afford to let these problems remain. If new potential customers got wind of these shenanigans many sales could be lost. A company must be pro-active when it comes to Customer Service. To wait until a problem develops may be too late—especially if the customer thought it should have been taken care of sooner.

In the following chapter, I have passed along some basic rules that should be followed in any kind of business. It was published many years ago and I hope the original writer doesn't mind, since he also copied it from the originators.

TQM—
Total Quality Management—

Originally written by Warren Berger, a free-lance writer from New York City.

When W. Edwards and Joseph Juran created total quality management, they developed 14 general principles to guide business. Here's how those principles translate into the language of real estate:

1.) **Create constancy of purpose to improve services.** Make sure everybody at your company shares the same goal of improving service. With input from field personnel and office staff, establish a quality mission statement.
2.) **Adopt the new philosophy of "quality first."** "Make quality conformance to consumers' requirements—the ultimate measure of success," says Gary Allhiser of Great Visions Consulting, an Arizona based TQM specialist.

3.) **Stop depending on inspections to achieve quality.** It's important to respond to complaints after the transaction, but you should also try to identify potential problems before they occur.
4.) **Stop awarding business on price tag alone.** Michael Bedworth, the former owner of Century 21—AAIM Realty, Inc., in Burke, VA. And now an associate broker at Long & Foster Real Estate in Fredericksburg, VA., suggests that you make recommendations about services on the basis of who will provide the best service to consumers.
5.) **Constantly improve your service systems.** As you begin to improve quality, don't become self-satisfied. You must keep listening to consumers and adapting to their changing wants and needs.
6.) **Institute training.** "Real estate companies generally don't do a good job of training salespeople." Says Atlanta based TQM consultant Martin Freedland. If you really want to establish a quality culture, back up your words with coursed, internally or externally, that'll teach the basics of quality management.
7.) **Institute leadership.** You must lead the way and set an example by providing quality service-good facilities, quick response to salespeople's needs, an open door policy, and so on.
8.) **Drive out fear.** Don't live in fear of temporary sales slumps. Focus on maintaining consistent quality performance that'll build consumer loyalty and produce sales down the road.
9.) **Break down barriers among staff areas.** Encourage teamwork among sales people and office staff toward the common goal of good customer service.

10.) **Eliminate slogans, exhortations and targets.** "Such things as arbitrary performance levels and ratios must be avoided in favor of reports showing increased customer satisfaction," says Allhister.
11.) **Eliminate numerical goals.** See Number 10.
12.) **Remove barriers to employees' pride in their work.** If you give staffers more freedom and authority and more of a say in company policies, everyone will have a stake in improving quality.
13.) **Institute a program for education and retraining.** Go beyond starter courses in quality management, then consider refresher courses to keep the momentum going.
14.) **Take action to accomplish the transformation.** Don't just talk about the quality. Do something about it.

(Words to build any successful business on)

In the following pages, I took the liberty of writing about my experiences with several companies, both large and small, and talking about their customer service—or lack of it. I'm sure all of you have experienced similar situations.

I've also given them a (*) star rating for that time when the problem situation occurred. They may be better—or worse today.

GE—
The General Electric Company—
* * *

Nearly every builder I have ever worked for ended up buying GE appliances for their new homes. I came to believe that they were the greatest ever built. I have to admit that during most of this time, only one salesman from GE came to call. He was GOOD. He knew his products and was able to offer very good deals. The contracts with GE generally just got renewed year after year, with the usual cost of living increases.

Don't get me wrong. I have nothing against General Electric products—except for an experience that happened in my last new house, after about four years of occupancy. We had had service on our new dishwasher after about two years, which cost about $175. I understand that since there are so many electronic components in nearly every appliance, the occasional break-down will occur. We didn't give that situation much thought.

However, after nearly four years, our upgraded microwave kept giving an F-4 reading whenever we used certain buttons. This was really annoying since we paid extra for all those buttons. It didn't seem to improve by itself, so a call was made to their service department. A date and time was arranged.

The day of the schedule, we received a call from the technician saying that he was going to order parts prior to coming out. This was understandable, since the previous service call was the same procedure. About a week later we received a call from GE service saying that they needed to schedule an appointment. Only one thing was wrong—the part(s) hadn't yet arrived. Once they did arrive, I arranged with them for a date and time.

The service representative couldn't find us on his sophisticated vehicle map and called us for information. Upon his arrival, I showed him the problem, and wouldn't you know, the F-4 didn't come on. Now the problem was two fold. Leave it alone and give the parts to the service rep., or repair it anyway with the new parts. The service rep. mentioned that he would hate to charge me a service call ($125) only to be called back again with an additional service call in a few days.

One thing you have to imagine. The parts (3) could be held in the palm of your hand, with your hand closed. It consisted of two different types of sensors and a probe. He spent about fifteen minutes changing the two sensors and asked about the probe. I said that our "old" probe seemed to be working just fine. He then said, "I'll give you credit for the probe." This probe is about eight inches long with one end fitting into a socket in the microwave and the other end into the meat. The credit was **$125.00**! At this point I was afraid to ask the prices on the two sensors he had just installed.

The total bill was **$387.52**! He said he wouldn't charge me for a service call—just to make me feel better. Then he asked if I was a "Senior Citizen." That really wasn't a thoughtful gesture on his part. We live in a senior community where you have to be 55+. This financial break allowed a 10% discount. Now the bill was around $355.00.

Now can you imagine if he had charged me a service call and the cost of the probe, it would have exceeded **$600.00**. We didn't pay that much for the entire microwave.

I have nothing against the service representative because he was pleasant and efficient. He also had a lap-top computer that has all the information needed, including the prices on every part.

Again, to make me feel better, he let me know that the new parts were guaranteed for 5 years. So if the replacement parts had a 5 year warranty, why didn't the parts they replaced?

I brought this question up with GE's *contact us* button on their web page. I haven't received a reply and the hopes of getting one are extremely slim. I did, however, look over their web page while I was there. It was quite impressive. They talked about all the good things they were doing and all the different types of industry they are involved with. They also mentioned that they grossed $41.6 BILLION during the 2nd quarter of 2005 and earning a profit of $4.6 BILLION. You can just bet that my $355 helped them gain this record profit.

Imagine for a moment how many appliances they sell in a year with parts that will give out in a short time. You can also imagine that any repairs have to be made by GE or the warranty is gone. Of course, nearly everything lasts one year, so that really isn't a big deal.

Out of curiosity, I looked for anything containing the words customer service. There wasn't any button to push to go to customer service. You had to use their search engine and then you came up with 9,468 times that customer service is mentioned. But, it really doesn't apply to you and me. It has to do more with; if you are having trouble with your jet engine, locomotive or power plant. The phone number—1-800-GE CARES—is a nice one, but do they really? Microwaves are just a dot on their company map and really don't add a whole lot to the bottom line—except, of course, the service department's share of the bottom line. It was stated that all 11 divisions had double digit improvement over the previous quarter. Now you know why they made monetary history.

I believe GE to be one of America's best companies. It's just too bad they feel they have to charge so much to repair their products. It's kind of like the computer printer business. They basically give the printer away but charge you an arm and a leg for the ink cartridge.

Ford Motor Company—
*

It really doesn't matter what period of time we are in. Bad customer service spans all time periods.

When I returned from overseas, during my stint in the US Air Force, I was in need of a vehicle. While I was away I decided that my present vehicle probably wouldn't serve my needs when I returned so I gave it to my dad to combine with his vehicle to trade in for something better for him. He traded both in and I was forced to use shanks ponies until I could find suitable transportation.

After an episode with the Chevrolet dealer, I decided to visit the local Ford dealership. A salesman had called my mother several days before to find out when I was coming home, so I thought I'd at least give him a chance.

I really liked the looks of the 1958 Ford Fairlane 500. It didn't take much effort on the salesman's part to convince me to buy. Things were going too easy. Now that I had my wheels all I had to do was find a girlfriend.

While I was cruising the town on my first night home with wheels, a loud squeal emanated from the motor. I couldn't imagine what could be wrong with my brand new car. I just knew that it needed to go back to the dealer right away.

The next morning I was at their doors explaining the problem. A mechanic came over and started to investigate. Of course you are invited to wait in their customer lounge while the service is being completed. Soon, my car was ready and it was good to not hear that terrible noise again. Little did I know, but I should have left it there at the dealer permanently.

That evening, as I continued my quest, the same noise reappeared. This really upset me and the next morning I went through the same procedure as the morning before.

This time I didn't visit the customer lounge and stayed to watch the progress. The noise was finally traced to a rocker arm and once it was removed, it was found to not have an oil groove on the inside. Therefore, it wasn't manufactured properly, but passed their rigid quality check. The mechanic didn't have one to replace it, but was able to grind a groove to allow the oil to flow. This took care of that problem.

I still had about fifteen months to serve in the Air Force and my next assignment was with an air traffic control mobile squadron out of Oklahoma City (Tinker AFB). This would require quite a bit of traveling and I had a brand new car to do it.

After an assignment back to Wisconsin, numerous trips home on weekends, back to Oklahoma City and finally being assigned to Vandenberg AFB near Lompoc, California, I had over 12,000 miles racked up. As you may recall, this mileage level was as high as automobile warranties went in those days. It was still less than one year old, but it was a one year OR 12,000 miles type warranty.

I started to notice that every time I checked the oil I was a quart or more low. I continued to observe where I parked, but spotted no puddles or other indication of an oil leak. I wrote Ford about this and their reply was that Sorry, but I could take it to the local dealer in Lompoc and if he needed any help in the repair that they would do so. It was now to the point that I was losing a quart of oil every 200 miles—give or take a few.

The dealer was sympathetic, but said he didn't have a clue to how to fix it and if I wanted to, I could leave it over there with those other two and wait for Ford to come up with a solution. He said that the design of the rear oil breather was faulty and the vacuum caused by driving at highway speeds actually sucked the oil right out of the engine. Now I had a brand new car that couldn't be driven at highway speeds.

I tried a make-shift solution to no avail. I stuffed steel wool up the breather tube hoping that it would break the suction process. I had always been told that F-O-R-D stood for Fix Or Repair Daily, but until now I really didn't believe it.

The fun of driving soon left me—at least with this car. I was soon to be released from service and just knew that I needed something more reliable. My Ford was just a little over one year old and I would look foolish trading it off at a loss. However, things have a way of working out to your benefit.

There was an independent auto dealer in Oklahoma City and as I was passing by one day I noticed that he had several odd looking small vehicles on the lot. They were called Volkswagen Beatles. These were actually "bootleg" vehicles and they still had the owner's manual in German. I fell in love with one, but he was curious why I would trade a great looking Ford in for a VW. My excuse was that I was getting married soon and I needed a more practical means of transportation. He seemed to understand that reasoning, but still stabbed me in the back on the deal.

Now I was the owner of a VW Beatle and he was the owner of a beautiful black, 2 door, Ford Fairlane 500 that had fatal problems. I'm sure he sold it quickly and probably as quickly started to receive complaints on his *steal deal*.

I've only owned one other Ford in my life and that was only a second car for short trips. That also was a "pile." Ford has never broken through to me again. It only takes one bad experience and it can last a lifetime.

Admiral Appliances—
* * *

Admiral, at one time at least, was a large name in the business. I first became aware of the name in the mid to late '60s. My partner and I (Distinctive Construction) each bought ourselves a new large, two door refrigerator/freezer. This was really a new concept and with our growing families, it was sure needed.

We both felt that we had the top of the line in refrigerators and were very pleased with our purchases. After all, this was about the only thing we would profit from one of our jobs. I guess we needed something solid to show for all our efforts.

Everything went fine for the first year or so. Like I mentioned before—everything lasts at least a year. Then we noticed that the ice cream was starting to run out the freezer door. A frantic call went in to their customer service and an appointment was set up. Several days later the repairman installed a new HEATER. I thought it already had a pretty good heater installed. After all, it melted the ice cream quite quickly.

This repair seemed to solve the problem—temporally. About every six to ten months after this repair, another needed to be scheduled. This time it seemed that there was a pressure leak, although minor, that over time drained the Freon and the unit again turned into a "heater."

One of the service personnel stated that the unit was designed to be under such high pressure that the slightest leak was sometimes very hard to find. The second to the last time, they sent two service personnel out and they took about four hours to go over the system from top to bottom to find and fix the leak.

The last time that a service person was called, and mind you this was about the sixth time, he stated that he couldn't work on it anymore unless I could prove the exact date when it was purchased. Apparently, his supervisor told him that six times was enough and to shine me on.

It took some doing, but I found the cancelled check from almost five years before (the warranty was for five years) and showed him. It still was about seven days from the five year mark and the service man called his supervisor.

There really wasn't much they could do except honor the warranty. So, the service man fixed it again—for the last time. We set about soon thereafter to locate another suitable refrigerator before this Admiral broke down again. We just knew that even if we paid Admiral out of our pocket they probably wouldn't come out again and we sure didn't want to be caught with rotten food.

Now Admiral knew that there was a problem with their design. In fact they changed it so there wasn't nearly the amount of pressure that our model had. But, they continued to patch up our refrigerator instead of really fixing the problem. I know they spent much more money on the repairs than the entire refrigerator cost in the beginning. This is a great example of bulling your way through regardless of what is the right, and most times, cost efficient thing to do. Kind of like—*"Damn the torpedoes, full steam ahead."*

Needless to say that Admiral didn't get anymore of our business from that time on. This is not to say that they didn't or don't produce good products. What it says is that *"You only have one chance to create a good first impression."*

Gateway Computer—
* *

Back in the 1990's, Gateway was an up and coming computer company with it's feet solidly stuck in cow manure back in Iowa— or someplace. You really got a good feeling about this company. Kind of like a small town boy growing up and making good.

I ordered a computer, which cost about $2,500, and I thought that the extended warranty would be a good idea. In case anything went wrong they would rush right out and fix it.

I had some problems with it and had spent many hours on the phone with their service desk. One thing that they couldn't seem to fix was the disk drive. For some reason it only worked when it wanted to and that wasn't very often. I wrote them about it and their reply was that I take the unit apart and then call them.

I had taken a computer apart before, but that was before I purchased insurance against having to do it again. I asked them when they were going to send someone out to fix it and their reply was that they would have to exhaust every other effort first which meant I was going to have to be the mechanic.

Needless to say, I did without that disk slot for the next several years. It didn't really bother me since floppies were still the standard method of recording.

It wasn't too long after that I started to read about Gateway having red quarters instead of black. They moved to Southern California and opened a lot of brick and mortar stores. The financial news was growing worse and the red ink was getting bigger.

One afternoon, a salesman from Gateway gave me a call to see if I was ready for a new computer. I asked him—"When are you going to fix my old one?" He wanted to know the whole story and told him that I would consider another one from them, if they would just fix my existing one. Then after about five minutes he said he couldn't help me and hung up.

The bad financial news continued and then there was the announcement that all the stores would close and they would, again, be moving. This truly is a company that had a good start but failed to follow through on their promises. I know the salespeople were under a lot of pressure to sell, but the layoffs came anyway. The company was heading downhill quickly and only a complete change in product, personnel and performance would save them. I really don't know how they are doing today, except I know some big changes have taken place. During this period of time, DELL® made their move and as of this writing, really don't have much competition. I bought one of their computers and haven't looked back since.

These companies that I have talked about here all have had good and bad periods in their growth. The people in charge now will not be the same ones ten years from now. Circumstances will change how a company operates, but customer service should *ALWAYS* be a priority. It doesn't matter who is in charge, the company *ALWAYS* needs customers and the best way to get them is to *KEEP* them.

Southwest Airlines—
* * * * *

I first became acquainted with Southwest when they started flying in and out of Orange County, John Wayne Airport. Their reputation preceded them as a cattle-call airline that had no frills.

While at a graduation ceremony in San Jose, California I noticed numerous funny colored Southwest planes preparing to land at the airport. It seemed like they were the only airline flying. One after another flew overhead.

Not to long after that I started working for the S•R Group and started a project in Northern California. Being associated with the customer service end of this project, I had to wait awhile before my turn at bat came up.

Soon I was told that frequent flights to the Oakland, California area would be coming up. I started traveling with my supervisor who would only fly on American or United. He considered Southwest far below his standards.

I noticed that being on time was not always a priority with American and United and also that their prices were fairly high for such a short flight.

Soon I was told that I would be flying alone, since he couldn't be away from the office so much. I started to book flights on Southwest, since their schedule seemed to fit mine much closer.

One thing I noticed with Southwest was that it was true that it was a cattle-call airline, but they did it so efficiently that it really was a pleasure to be a *cattle* for the day. They not only handled more passengers per employee, but they seemed to do it with more ease and friendliness.

I always arrived at the ticket check-in counter early because I wanted the number one boarding ticket—if possible. Since Southwest did not have assigned seating, that meant that you were first to board, right after children and others that needed assistance. I usually sat in the same seat both up and down the state. Not only did this give me the best view, but it was close to the front, which made it easier to get off. It was also on the opposite side of the sun both coming and going. This made for a much more pleasant ride.

While waiting for the check-in counter to open (Southwest opened one hour prior to scheduled take-off) I couldn't help but notice the other half of the counter was occupied by American West Airlines. They had a flight scheduled to take-off at 7:00 AM—the same time that Southwest was to open their portion of the counter.

American West would have three and four people behind the small counter checking in passengers and several people taking their tickets to board. The line seemed a mile long and moving very slowly.

Both airlines flew the same capacity plane. American West's plane was at the airport overnight while the Southwest plane was due to arrive from Oakland (to Orange County) at 7:30. This meant that the gate was shared with one-half hour in between. It also meant that American West had to make room for Southwest. It shouldn't have been a problem.

But—many times the five or six American West personnel couldn't get their passengers on board prior to the Southwest planes arrival. Many times they had to move their plane to another gate to complete loading.

While all this confusion was going on we would now have two long lines waiting to be checked in. The big difference was that Southwest had ONE person behind the counter and ONE person taking boarding cards. And, Southwest's line was moving noticeably faster. Several times our 8:00 AM departure beat out their 7:00 AM flight.

More people flying, more planes arriving and departing and fewer people to handle the load. How does this work? Mainly by prioritizing needs. Passengers want to leave on time and arrive on time. For an hours flight you don't need unnecessary frills, you need efficiency and courtesy. Southwest figured that out and practiced it on every one of their flights.

Peanuts and a beer, wine or soda was all that was available. I think they had some hard liquor as well. By the time they had that passed out, the plane was in the landing pattern at your destination, generally on-time.

Another perk is their frequent flyer program. Eight round trips—anywhere they fly—and you get a free round trip pass—to anywhere they fly. That meant that flying back and forth to Oakland from Orange County eight times—which is about their shortest flight—I could now fly to and from the East coast, or wherever they fly, for free.

Just recently (2005) many airlines are having financial trouble. American West merged with U.S. Airways which is a combining of losers. Both were either in or facing bankruptcy at the merger time. Many are canceling flights due to the recent, drastic increase in fuel costs. Some how, Southwest has managed to make a profit every quarter. I wonder if there is a lesson to be learned there?

These are just a few stories about some companies that I have experienced the bad and the good customer service. There are many other stories to be told, but I'm sure the point has been made.

All companies need to be reminded that to stand still is to fall back. You have to continually move forward just to stay even.

Dell Computer—
* * * *

I believe Dell to be one of those good companies that could become great. Their ads are everywhere and their products seem to be selling quickly.

I now have purchased two computers from Dell. Both were nearly bare-bones with only moderate upgrades. My first purchase went very smooth, however, the second was a real struggle.

The second one was a purchase for my mother-in-law who just wanted to get more familiar with the internet and email. Nothing was special with this order, except that the offer came with a "free printer."

I like to buy things on the internet because I don't have to talk with any salesperson and argue about what I need and what they think I need. This internet sale went well, except for the fact that when I received my printed out order I didn't see any "free printer" listed. This caused me great concern since I know that items not listed just do not show up in the shipping box.

Dell had a customer service number listed for information about orders and so I gave it a try. I did notice that the extension part of the number was quite long, but didn't think too much about it. Soon a person came on the line that really had trouble with the English language and sort of mumbled her words. It was extremely hard to understand her, but the gist of her remarks was that Dell did NOT have a *free printer promotion* with that computer.

Now I was really upset because I clicked on the computer picture that had the sign, "Includes free printer," on it. She was insistent however and she hung up on me. I know that many companies are farming out their customer service to foreign countries, such as; India and the Philippines. I only hope they test out this system carefully since it still is very hard to understand these people and when you're dealing with a real problem you need good communication. Now I know why the phone number had such a long extension with it. I was calling half way around the world. Now I had to find another path to vent my anger.

I now emailed their local customer service. I had told them of the problem that I hadn't received the free printer with my order. I received a response the next day telling me that Dell did NOT have a free printer offer with that computer. I again checked my order and also the morning paper and they both had listed the computer I purchased with a free printer. I again sent an email back and said that I don't know what they were looking at, but my TV and my newspaper listed that computer with a free printer and I expected the order to include the printer.

They emailed me back to again inform me that it still wasn't offered, BUT since I was a *valued customer* they would send me the free computer as soon as my computer order was shipped. They gave me a reference number and asked me to email them just as soon as the computer was shipped.

Several days later, I was notified that the computer order was shipped. I immediately emailed them the reference number and was informed that the printer would ship the following day.

This may seem trivial, but if they can get that worked up over a $79 printer, just think what would happen if it would have been more expensive.

I still don't see their side of the argument. They were still advertising the free printer a month later. Could it be that their advertising department doesn't tell anyone else in the company what is going on? I do know that it took someone who spoke good English and with a clear understanding of the different nomenclature of their products.

This also points out the fact that you cannot just hire someone to sit in the customer service seat and solve problems. Also, you cannot just hire people that already have trouble speaking your language to satisfactorily discharge disagreements. It may cost less to farm out this portion of the business, but at what cost will it really be? There are quite a few computer companies bidding for your business and the customer surely doesn't have to put up with screwed up service representatives.

Farmer Boys—
(World's Greatest Fastaurant)
* * * * ½

One cannot leave out smaller companies when looking at customer service. We recently had a new Farmer Boys restaurant built close to us and have only gone there about three times since it opened.

Our first impression was that it was clean. Naturally, all new restaurants are probably clean. So we were a little skeptical until we tasted their food.

We went back again and were really surprised that their menu was fairly extensive. It, apparently, was always extensive, but we just never got past the hamburger part of the menu. It was about dinner time and we decided to order a meal and not just a hamburger.

It was delivered to our table by a server and we were taken back by the size of the offering. The steak and shrimp were of such size to fill the hungriest person and the price was really small compared to the size.

We again went back several weeks later and ordered sandwiches that, again, were large for the price. During the meal, the Shift Supervisor came by to ask how we liked everything and gave us a card to go online to take a short survey. Many established fast food places don't feel they need to take surveys anymore.

When we arrived back home, I immediately went on-line and completed the short survey. It only took about five minutes to complete, but they wanted to know how they were doing in a number of areas. One, of course, was the quality of their food. Another was the quality of their staff.

On a scale of 1 to 5, with 5 being the best, I gave all the questions a 5. I don't think any other fast food outlet would garner more than a 3 in most categories. First, the order taker was of Mexican decent, but spoke nearly perfect English and was thoroughly informed about the products she sold as well as being very pleasant. Then we noticed that the people taking care of the dirty dishes were also very pleasant. They also spoke very good English.

Knowing that in today's fast food market, some stores are farming out their order takers to foreign countries. How in the world they can make that happen at a lower cost is beyond me. Imagine talking to someone in India or the Philippines after the initial "may I take your order?" Then to have that information arrive back to the kitchen, which is only five feet away; at a faster rate than talking to someone that is only three feet away.

This generally boils down to the fact that the owners/managers do not take the time to train their staff or feel that they are beyond training. At least in those other countries the people that have these jobs are trying to understand the English language. Here in America, so many have mangled the language that they may be beyond help. They still expect top wages, but fail to improve themselves.

This does not seem to be the problem at Farmer Boys. Although many seemed to be of Mexican decent, all that came into contact with the buying public were extremely pleasant and spoke very good English.

It is indeed a pleasure to find great customer service in smaller companies. You basically expect it in larger ones—those that really can afford it—but when a small company really stands out it needs to be noted.

I hope that this analysis applies to all their stores. I've only visited one other before and that was sometime ago and it didn't strike me as something really special.

If I have a choice now, I will visit this Farmer Boys whenever possible.

In the following pages, I've included some newspaper articles I recently found in my local paper. They tell a lot about the condition of customer service in this country.

News Articles—

July 26, 2005—The Press-Enterprise—Moreno Valley Edition.
EarthLink plans to cut customer-service jobs:
About 180 EarthLink employees in Atlanta will lose their jobs as the Internet provider completes a move to outsource customer service and technical support telephone lines.

EarthLink cut 1,300 call center employees in 2003 and another 1,300 in 2004 as it began farming out the work to call centers in India and the Philippines.

The job cuts will take place between August and September. EarthLink will be left with 1,020 employees in Atlanta and 1,800 nationally.

NEW YORK TIMES NEWS SERVICE

The very next day the following occurred—

EarthLink sees decline in dial-up subscribers:
Internet-service provider EarthLink Inc. on Tuesday posted a 12 percent drop in second quarter profit, hurt by falling revenue as subscribers moved away from its premium dial-up service.

> *Stifled by tough competition and greater demand for high speed connections, EarthLink said its customer rolls could worsen by the end of this year amid a waning market for dial-up access.*
>
> *The company, however, is hoping to offset its shrinking ISP business with new offerings that will drive future growth.*
>
> *In the latest three-month period, income fell to $43.8 million or 31 cents per share, from $49.7 million, or 31 cents a year ago. The per-share figures reflect a greater number of shares outstanding in the latest period.*
>
> THE ASSOCIATED PRESS

Now that's what I call fast action. First they announce a change in their customer service policy and the very next day they discover the loss of hundreds of customers. I'm sure it didn't just happen in one day. But, you can see that problems have been going on for some time and they just came to a head. Had the news articles been reversed, as to when they appeared, it would look like the sagging number of customers caused the company to send jobs overseas. However, I believe that the company's knee-jerk reaction caused great concern to their customers and they responded accordingly.

Customers get tired of paying the high price that once was standard in the Internet supplier business when so many others are coming out with higher speed connections at a much reduced rate. This is an example of—"it was good enough then and it's good enough now." Stand still and you will actually be going backwards.

Another news article appeared in my local paper on October 2, 2005 under the heading—**Good Jobs, Sans College—No flash but the pay's OK and they'll be here awhile:**

Customer service representative—Income range: $20,960 to $33,540. Projected annual openings: 74,137. High school or college, plus training provided by employers is required. Communications skills matter.

The work—answering customers' questions in person, on the phone or via e-mail or the Internet—is stressful. The turnover rate is often high and off-shoring is possible.

You can see that the requirements for the position require very good communication skills. Why then do companies feel they need to send this business to foreign countries? TO SAVE MONEY!

They are not really interested in how the customer perceives this move, but rather how their financial bottom line looks at the end of the year.

They also may be thinking that these foreign countries are working harder to teach their people how to speak English than this country is. So many younger people can't put two words together to make sense. Even Bill Cosby gets upset at listening how young people talk. How are they going to talk to an earlier generation that, at least, tried to learn their communication skills? You can see that companies do not want to teach these younger people something that they refused to learn in school or just weren't taught properly from the start.

Many college graduates cannot write a short story that makes any sense at all. Some of these same students may earn millions of dollars in sports, but when interviewed about their heroics on the field, come off like a fifth-grader just learning to speak in sentences. It's really a disgrace, but maybe this is a subject for another book.

Lip Service—

Another well known builder, who at the time was one of the leading builders in the USA, had the fastest building schedule around. The Supt. had less than sixty days to complete a home and have the buyer move in. If you couldn't keep up that schedule, you might be looking for another job quickly. So much had to do with their public image since every three months they had to show good numbers for their investors. This meant that every quarter the company had to start from scratch and better itself every three months.

Now you might assume that with 20+ working days each month, this could be accomplished—with luck. A friend of mine, who was a superintendent for them, said that everyone knew when they had to finish, but most times had trouble knowing the start date. This, of course, led to high anxiety and shoddy workmanship when eventually given the green light.

Now the schedule turned to twelve hour days and seven days a week just to make this happen. This did not foster good customer service. Items that should have been built better weren't given the right amount of time to get it done and were passed off as industry standards.

My supervisor at the company I worked for at the time bought a two story home, from this builder, with a great view, but with numerous problems. He had asked me to go through the house in the framing stage and before the walk-through to give him an idea as to the quality of construction. It was quite evident that the reputation of this builder was truly coming out in this home and there were a number of items to discuss.

Then after moving in, more items came up for their customer service department to investigate. Usually, one would come out and look at the problems and then get on the radio and tell someone to come over a fix it. Apparently his radio didn't work because no one showed up and the matter had to be recalled.

Usually after doing this several times you either gave up or exploded. Now you have to act like you will go all the way with a law suit or forget it altogether. If it is something small, but irritating, you might be better off to forget it. If it is something significant, you needed to be prepared to do battle over a fairly long period of time.

A friend of mine, who was my customer service manager on a project, eventually worked for this builder as their customer service manager. He became so frustrated that he couldn't take it any longer and had to tell them what they could do with the job. He was a great manager, but their policies were that it was cheaper to go to court than give good service. This same builder had to change their name (again) to give the appearance that new ideas and new management came to the forefront. Actually it was to allow them to continue to stay in business while the old company was getting it's behind sued off.

This company continues to do business; however, they no longer hold the number one spot. They had to make some very basic changes to their company policies and word has it that it is a much better company to work for and buy from. However, their reputation is still out there and it will be some time before that will change—no matter how much better they are.

By the Book—

One of the first jobs for the builder, upon turning over a house to a buyer, is to hand them a homeowner's manual. These can be bought from many different book stores—especially those that deal in construction manuals, etc. You can also purchase a computer disk that you can use to make your own copies. This is called a *boiler plate* and many times has to be revised considerably to have any correlation with what you are building. Many smaller builders only know how to put their name on the cover, but fail to read the inside.

Don't get me wrong. There is nothing wrong with using one of these. You must take out the items that do not apply and insert new ones that do. Nothing is more frustrating to a new home owner to read all about keeping water out of a basement when you don't have one. Nor does it make sense to have paragraphs describing how to keep snow off the roof when you live in the desert.

The homeowner manual should be the *bible* by which judgments are made. However, many times, the problems lie somewhere in-between the judging rules and it takes a well versed person to make the proper decision. Generally the cost of the correction is quite small, but many service people believe the reward to be great to be able to say no and save the company that money. Many service people would rather spend hours battling with a customer to save ten bucks than to spend it quickly and gain the customers thanks.

Once the customer believes they have to battle you for the least little item, you have lost the gratitude of the buyer. Now you really can't do enough to please them, no matter how much you do or how quickly you do it. They generally continue to complain over the least problem and give you a list a mile long. They really aren't interested in getting all their items completed. They are actually punishing you for your treatment of them in the past.

Customer Trust—

A customer's trust is something that is easily lost and almost impossible to gain back. I have a note pad that has a reminder on every page that says, *"It may take months to find a new customer—but only seconds to lose one."* This is so true. However, most builders will spend thousands to sell a product and at the same time cut their customer service budget to pay for it. They will also spend thousands on lawyers and then hire the cheapest subcontractors around. Kind of backwards if you ask me.

On my second day as Director of Construction, with The William Lyon Company, (I was also responsible for customer service), I was asked to solve a customers' problems that was causing the service manager fits. The prior occupant of my position had told him to tell the customer NO. The customer continued to bring up his list of ten items and threatened to picket the sales office to get his way.

The service manager and I met the homeowner and went over his list. Only one item would cost anything besides an hour or so with a good service person. That item was estimated to cost $100 to fix. I asked the owner, "Which item is the one that is really making you mad?" He said that the one that was going to cost $100 was the one because he truly felt that it wasn't his fault that the vinyl floor was torn and it was that way when they moved in. He also said that he really didn't care about the other nine.

I told him that not only would we replace the flooring, but we would also fix the other nine items on his list. So for $100 and an hours worth of a service person's time, we solved the problem.

Several weeks later he called and apologized for disturbing me, but one thing still wasn't taken care of on his list. It was a rain gutter, that when viewed from his stairs looking out a window, appeared to be crooked. He said that every time he walked down the stairs it really bothered him. I immediately sent over the service manager and he made sure it was taken care of. We never heard from him again and we put his name in the satisfied customer side of the ledger.

To gain the customer's trust you need to be pro-active. When I needed to correct a structural framing problem that occurred in 87 homes, over half of which were occupied, the thought came to mind that the problem might go away if I did nothing. But knowing that it doesn't work that way, I recalled all the occupied homes to fix this problem.

The framer, engineer and I came up with a solution that could be basically pre-cut and easily assembled in the homeowner's attic in a short time. The next step was gaining acceptance from the building department.

They had never heard of a builder recalling homes to fix something, especially this many homes and with people living in them as well. They had no objections to the fix and said they would let any homeowners know that it had been approved if they happen to call and inquire.

This all happened just as the weather was getting hot so the scheduling needed to be made early in the morning before the attic heated up too much. This was accomplished in about six weeks and no one had called the building department. Only one person called the office and asked what was done, since he was in the attic and couldn't see what new item was added. If that person hadn't been in the attic before the fix, they sure couldn't tell what we added to make their home safer. This was a pro-active move on our part and thoroughly impressed both the homeowners and the building department. The problem that would have come up, if a structural failure had occurred, would have still been our fault, even though the building department had passed all 87 homes. A law suit of this magnitude would have made the difference between a profitable project and a loser.

Another test of customer trust came shortly after the above incident. Our service department always kept one key from a set of ten so that they could get back in, prior to the owner moving in, to complete the walk-through repairs. When you have over three hundred homes in a project, this adds up to a lot of keys.

As I was coming to work one morning, my car phone rang and it was my customer service field manager. He hated to tell me, but during the night, someone broke in the customer service trailer and stole all the keys. It took me a few minutes to get my heart from coming out of my chest and I asked him if I could call him back once I reached the office. During the short remaining drive, I came up with the beginnings of a plan that I thought might work. I ran it by him and we set it in motion.

He knew a reliable locksmith in the area and talked with him about the problem. We had about 150 homes that someone had a key to and what would it cost to re-key five locks each with new keys. It worked out a little easier than that. We were able to switch locks from one phase to another and from one end of the project to the other. But it was still a logistics nightmare. We could have not said anything and hoped for the best, but, again, if the truth got out—and it surely would—the company would have had BIG problems on their hands from a big number of homeowners.

Again, being pro-active saved the day. The homeowners were thankful that we cared enough to go to all that trouble. Needless to say, the strict rules about not keeping customer keys were energetically enforced.

Who's Responsible?—

There is only one answer to this question. The Boss—The Owner—The CEO or whoever occupies that big corner office with all the windows. The one who is answerable to the shareholders, the one that signs the checks or the one that gives all the orders is the one who must be responsible. Everyone else is in a support position and can only carry out the company policies.

Those that are in the top position may delegate authority to someone else, but they cannot delegate responsibility. If the policies do not come from the "top" they will surely fail and it will still be the big cheeses' fault.

Some of the companies that I worked for had very little policy coming down from the top to indicate how customer service is to be handled. One of their biggest policies was to save money wherever possible. This policy was supreme and all other policies were subservient to it. If you came up with a better idea to handle customer service, the inevitable response was that we had to save money—even if it didn't cost anything more.

Most builders are spendthrifts on advertising or ego building, but penny pinchers when it comes to customer service. They look at customer service as an expense and not as an investment. The more that is spent on the customer service operation—the less can be spent on advertising. Believe me; a favorable word of mouth is much more effective and less costly.

The builder needs to look at his rising advertising budget as a very good indication that he is really lacking in the customer service department. The only bad thing about actually realizing this and trying to reverse it—is that it will take time to have this move show results. Again, *"It may take months to find a customer, but only seconds to loose one."* If you can't take the time to turn things around, you might have to change your name and start over like many companies have already done.

Customer service needs to be implemented and have staying power within the company. If you start a new policy for great service and not give it a chance to grow, you will do more harm than good. There has to be a track record established to really start paying off. It's kind of like—*"give a person a fish and you feed him for a day—teach a person to fish and you feed him for life."* The longer great customer service is the company policy the more this reputation spreads.

I spent four years working on it with The William Lyon Company. They already had a pretty good reputation when it came to the quality of their product, but combining that with great customer service made the product even better. This is a combination that every company needs to aspire to. A great product and great service will reward the company for many years to come.

Even if the product is at the high end of the scale, business will continue. I just read that Nordstrom was, again, enjoying a great profit quarter.

Quality builders with quality products and quality service will have business even in a recession. That is when those that have money like to spend it. They believe they get the most bang out of their investment. These people will spread the word faster to their money friends than any amount of advertising.

One company that I worked for (The Konwiser Corporation) I had never heard of. I had never viewed one of their ads in the paper nor knew anything about what they built. I went back to my previous company to get some information and all they could say was that, "it seems like when building is down, they always are working." That was the best information I could possibly receive. I didn't care what they built as long as they built. This is also the company that I spend over one quarter of my career with. This is also the company that really started my path to providing great customer service.

How to Change—

Again—change has to come from the top. If the boss just gives the order to change then all you can expect is a temporary new course direction and soon it will be back to the old status quo. Heads may roll, but not only the direction needs to come from the top, but also inspiration, confirmation, authentication, motivation and encouragement need to follow. If these are missing, the person in charge of carrying out these orders will feel like being at the end of a limb and hearing the chain saw start up.

A person designated to carry out great customer service MUST be empowered to do it. This can be a stretch for some companies. To willingly give some one the power to spend money without getting all sorts of okays first just can't be done in some companies. This person may feel like they have the empowerment, but then the first time they try it and are called on the carpet for it, will kill that feeling forever. Mistakes will be made, but puncturing the empowerment balloon is the worst thing that can happen. That person may never again feel comfortable giving great service.

The change that came from the top in The William Lyon Company was a success because the empowerment also came along with it. You would more than likely be called on the carpet if you didn't use your empowerment. Word spread quickly when great service was preformed. When a 17 year owner's family bought another house after suing the company and loosing, when the lawsuits diminished to nearly nothing, when approval ratings hovered around the top spot for years and when division personnel were really excited about coming to work was the time when you realized that something was being done right. That something was the customer service policy implemented from the top.

This policy didn't just pertain to our customers, but to our fellow employees and subcontractors as well. After all, these also are our customers. Everyone we deal with or do business with needs to be treated as our customers. Now the word really gets out and spreads quickly. Now the quality of your products also increases just because you treat people differently than other companies.

Once this new policy does come down to be implemented, there needs to be someone who truly believes in this new policy. If you place an old school person in charge, the results will not be satisfactory. This person is more willing to give lip service to the new policy and continue to do the same thing as before. Now it will take months and possibly years before the lack of progress in noticed. Now the company has lost it's zeal for the new policy and will revert back to the "old ways." The hands-on person just has to be on-board with the new policy. There is no substitution for direction from the top.

The next level personnel also must be on the same page. The people that truly meet the customer must have the knowledge and encouragement to satisfy the customer's complaint and put that customer of the plus side of the ledger. If they give off negative vibes or promise things that can't be done, they are a negative to the company and must be re-educated or dismissed. You don't have to accept a set of tires for credit, like Nordstrom, to give great service. But, you have to be honest, listen, act positively, and follow-through just like you would want done to you.

Personnel—

The quality of personnel can not be underestimated. Customer service personnel need to be the cream of the crop, the best of the best and bubbling over with knowledge and personality. They can not be left-over construction people, the assistant superintendent, or some friend that wants you to give him a job. They can not be someone you can hire at a cheap rate and pretend your service problems are over. This person deals with YOUR customers and leaves with them a lasting impression as to the quality of your company.

Whether they are assigned phone duty or actually fixing something, they must be the best at it that you can find. They must also look the part of a professional person that you would trust with the reputation of your company—because that's what you must do! You are putting a sign around their neck saying—*I represent my company and I speak for the boss.* If you don't think they can do that, you need to keep looking.

At The William Lyon Company I had about 75% great service people and about 25% good service people. We tried to match up their abilities and personality with the right type of project. That is to say—some service people are much more comfortable with a certain level of buyers. Others may be more sophisticated and are able to work with higher end buyers. It is important to do your best to match them up so that both the service person and the customer feel good about the relationship.

If a high end buyer is given the feeling that the service is not quite up to par in every respect, they will spread the word fast and the service person will find resentment from the whole community. This may not have anything to do with their ability to fix something, or their work habits, but could stem from their outward appearance or their manner of speaking.

A service worker that comes into your home with dirty clothes on will not be offered to sit anywhere and will be watched to make sure none of the dirt comes off their clothes. It also usually indicates a messy work habit. Instead of using a rag to wipe their hands they may just wipe them on their pants or shirt. Of course this isn't always the case. There are many service jobs that require getting dirty. However, you need to change your image before going to the next job. A spare set of clothes, with you, will always come in handy.

A word about *older* employees needs to be emphasized here. So many companies are looking at their older employees and thinking that they will soon have to do something about them. That something is usually finding ways to ease them out of their position, which has to be done with a strong reason so the company can't be sued for discrimination, and get someone younger to replace them.

I was once told that some companies get rid of their older employees and hire two younger ones in their place. This has to do only with saving money. It is very short sighted and actually very stupid; as witnessed in an article in AARP—The Magazine in the Nov. /Dec. 2005 issue under the heading "Working Wonders" by Brad Edmondson.

"They're dependable, caring, experienced, and wise. And that's just for starters. So it's no surprise that more and more smart companies are turning to older workers to get the job done right."

What's the big attraction? "People in their 50s and 60s have a great work ethic, and they want to spend time with customers," explains Kay Jackson, a spokesperson for RadioShack. "We want people who are passionate about customer service..."

Companies need to realize that they have spent so much into the training of that older worker that it would be money ahead to keep them and not have to lay out more money to train a younger new one.

Training—

A service person's supervisor needs to observe actual fixing sessions. If the service worker has the mentality that all it takes is a bigger hammer, bears watching and training. I know that sometimes you can smack a cabinet door or tweak the hinges, or adjust something with your foot, but you need to know when these techniques can be applied. If the owner/buyer is standing right there and watching your every move, a more sophisticated approach needs to be used. And—if your service technician doesn't posses that type of approach, they need to be trained or taken off the job.

I once had a service representative that was very personable and gave the air of knowing how to fix anything. This occurred while working on apartments and most everyone loved him. He was long on personality, but quite short on work expertise.

He replaced many tile floors with vinyl 12" x 12" tiles. However, very seldom did the tiles line up. It gave the odd feeling that you were walking crooked when you entered the kitchen. He didn't think lining up the tile was important. After all, these were apartments and he had to do the job fast. Another example of his lack of expertise was where he needed to replace an electrical plug. He pulled out the broken plug, cut the wires and stuck them into the new plug. The problem was that he didn't bother to notice how they came out or how they should go in the new one. The dead plug was again reported as a problem, but this time, my son who was quite proficient in electricity, fixed the problem. The service person had EVERY wire stuck in the wrong slot. The funny part was that the plug had the wiring instructions right on the back.

We tried everything to help bring him around to doing more things right, but he had reached his limit. One of his favorite fixes had to do with a drywall patch in a wall where the door knob busted a hole. His first action was to find something to stuff in the hole. This could be paper, a soda can or some other item. Next he would slap on a large glob of drywall mud and smooth it over. Once it hardened, he would paint it and leave. Of course, the very next time the door hit the same spot, the same problem occurred and the same fix was applied. Eventually the wall looked so bad that a large section had to be cut out and professionally repaired.

One good thing about our crew with The Konwiser Corporation was that we did have some service people with professional abilities. Many had numerous abilities that I would match with anyone in the business. Over time, there wasn't much that our service department couldn't handle.

We started classes to inform those that didn't know or were a little rusty in the drywall trade. Our expert would demonstrate in our storage room and then help the others try it out. Everyone enjoyed the learning process, except the one that had already reached his learning capacity. He was embarrassed and didn't want the others know that he was really thin on drywall knowledge. They all knew his deficiencies so we even tried private lessons, but that still would have been an admission that he really needed the training. It wasn't long after that he became dispensable. Of course, we all are dispensable, but it shouldn't be for those reasons.

One of the best ways to train someone is to have them follow someone that knows how to do it. When operating *Home Team* we would have some selected personnel follow along on a walk-through to see how it is done.

When we (*Home Team*) first started with one builder, I took the first walk-through and was watched by the customer service director. After about 30 minutes and apparently satisfied with what she saw and heard, she left. It's not easy having someone watch you, but you should get used to it. There were numerous times that I would be asked to handle some "tough" customers. Sales would tell us that these owners were really hard to get along with and to be on our guard. I found, almost without exception, that dealing honestly and pleasantly with the customer usually dispelled the applied reputation. Also, if they feel you know what you are talking about, you have a much better chance of having a pleasant experience.

While I was with National Builders Service, (*Home Team*), we actually started P & D University. This wasn't an accredited school of higher learning by any means, but rather we were fulfilling the basic needs required for a *prep and detail* person. This is a person that basically goes into a house, generally before the walk-through, to do the minor touch-up and repairs that usually end up on the walk-through list. This is actually an art. You may have to caulk, paint, adjust, clean, replace, and repair any number of items in a house.

The person that does this really needs to know all the angles to do it with any proficiency. Old school construction people usually do not qualify for this occupation. Their philosophy is the bigger hammer approach. The real P & D person is like a surgeon using his scalpel and leaving no scar. Just watching them is an experience.

Naturally, this kind of experience can only be obtained through countless trial and error sessions. You cannot teach someone, in one week, everything about being a professional prep and detail person. What we tried to do was to have them jump start their abilities so they wouldn't have to spend months or years getting to know the basics. There were some students that were very excited when they were able to run a continuous bead of caulk without it oozing all over the place. That was progress. Sound simple? Try it.

Some students felt the whole process was beneath them and wanted more of the manager type position. Even though they didn't have the qualifications, they knew the pay was better and that was their goal in life. Cut out the middle positions and go right to the top.

We set up wall sections so they could get some practice patching drywall holes. This takes lots of practice, over time, but we didn't have the time. Small holes they could handle, but some of the larger ones were left for the "teachers."

We had a variety of students. Some were hiding from the law, some were single mothers and some were lazy. The one hiding from the law was a good student and within a couple of weeks obtained a position with a builder, only to have that fall apart the night before starting. He was arrested and spent some time in jail. I don't know what happened after that.

One fairly young mother of three drove about 75 miles each way, every day, just to learn the trade. She was so excited the day she learned how to caulk properly that she spent hours that night, at home, doing caulking. The next morning she came bouncing in and told me all about her experience. If all the students had this kind of enthusiasm, teaching would be lots of fun.

Supervision—

If your supervisor is just a friend that needs a job, or a family member that you feel some responsibility for, or someone that is kicked upstairs for some reason—you have the wrong person. A supervisor needs to be one that has a good grasp on all aspects of customer service. From the messy part of fixing something, to knowing how to talk to customers, to knowing how to motivate and instruct those he/she is supervising. This person needs to know when to step forward and correct and when to stay back and allow mistakes. They need to know when to criticize and when to praise, when to promote and when to hold back.

The same traits that are found in a great CEO need to be found in those placed in charge. Although this may not be found in the same quantity as a good CEO, but it still needs to be present.

This part of middle management is extremely important to larger companies. Without this entity it would just be someone giving orders and someone trying to fulfill them. If you hire young, inexperienced workers to carry out the orders, you better have someone capable of interpreting them for the worker.

While working for The Konwiser Corporation, I had the opportunity to visit a seminar that the boss was giving at UCLA in Los Angeles. During the question and answer period, someone asked him how he was able to handle so many young and inexperienced workers in his building. He answered, as he looked up at me, that he had an old man also there showing them the way. I didn't know whether to feel good or bad at his comment. After all, I am still three years younger that he is, but I was the oldest worker at the time.

He also stated once that while flying back home, he met another builder on the plane and they started talking. This other builder gave out his secret for keeping costs in check. *"Fire the older and more expensive guys and hire two younger ones in their place."* We were told this philosophy later and also told that "not to worry—it wouldn't happen in his company." It's surprising how things like this can stick in a person's mind. If a buck needs to be made, there are many ideas that come to mind and this is one of them.

Middle management is usually the first place that cut-backs are started. The guys are trained well enough now—don't you think? The problem is that some of the guys never get past their training. There are always new and puzzling problems arising that needs the expertise of great middle management. A middle manager not only has experienced many—many different scenarios, but also has the ability to deal successfully with new ones.

Completing 73 town homes in 15 days from framing to finish—including common area amenities like two hand ball courts inside a new recreation building, swimming pool and spa, plus sidewalks and landscaping was one of those new scenarios. Also, in 19 days, completing 34 apartments starting with the framing, including pool and laundry, sidewalks and landscaping, carports and paving was another new scenario. I don't know of any two-for-one personnel swaps that could have filled that requirement.

If you as a builder, buyer or customer ever face a very young, seemingly still wet behind the ears and not really sure of what he is saying, customer service supervisor, be very careful. I'm not putting down youth, but you are not born with customer service experience. You have to earn that and that takes time and it usually shows on the person's face. Those lines and deep seated eyes only reflect the abuse and sometimes hatred they have been through.

As an example; One day I needed to take my company car into the dealer for service. I was told that it would be ready at 5:00 PM which was perfect. I rented a vehicle and at the days end arrived back at the dealer. I then was told that my vehicle hadn't been completed yet. Actually, it hadn't been touched yet. I was told not to worry because they were open until 9:00 PM that night and it would be completed by then. At the appointed hour, I arrived and waited. Out came a very young man who had the duty of telling me that it still hasn't been touched, but they definitely would have it completed the next day.

I don't know everything I said to that young man, but none of it was pretty. My voice could be heard all over the agency and I know that the customer service "supervisor" was within ear shot. However that person thought best not to come out and just let the young guy get yelled at. The owner of the agency called me the next day an apologized profusely, but the damage had already been done.

There was a proper way of handling this problem, but they didn't find it. They were short mechanics that day and overloaded them. Instead of letting me know the truth at 5:00 PM and very possible paying for a rental car for the next day they perpetuated the mistake once again to 9:00 PM and then not even offering to pay for the next day's rental. This isn't just poor service—its immature service. Bad things can happen every day in every business. It's how you take care of business that counts.

Monitoring Results—

Monitoring the results of your customer service computer program, your surveys and general word of mouth is the second most important step to take. The first most important step is, of course, actually starting your computer program and surveys.

Many builders spend good money to install various programs and institute different surveys and then not take the time to analyze the results. As long as one home owner says they like the product, seems to satisfy the builder.

This data is extremely important to the welfare of the company. How this information is used may well decide the health of the company for the near future. This is like reading a road map. If you know what you're looking at—you're not lost. If you don't—you are.

Most builders rely on their own progress monitoring system. This usually consists of one or two customers saying they like the product and taking that to represent everyone else. Builders are afraid of criticism and will find it hard to lay out good money to possibly get a truckload of it back.

The one company (The William Lyon Company) that did the best job at monitoring their progress hired an outside firm that was experienced in setting up a great customer service program and obtaining the results. Tom Callister's Resource Management and

Marketing Solutions did an excellent job in providing the solutions to great service and another company did the surveying. We received survey results quarterly on all our projects. There was one other division that did the same. However, several other divisions felt that they didn't have enough products to enter into the survey.

Our division (Central Counties Division) came in second in the overall ratings compared to twenty other builders. These were based on many aspects of the building and buying experience. Everything was rated from the initial sale, escrow, through customer service.

Not only was our product under the microscope, but many of our personnel were also. Our rating of number two was considered to be a great achievement. The builder who usually came in number one (although we never knew his name) was much smaller than we were. He completed about forty to sixty homes per year (that much we did know) and our division alone completed up to 675 homes per year.

To have that volume and that high a rating was considered remarkable. The other division in the company gave more lip service to all this newfangled customer service and basically did things the way they were always done. However, even they were able to reach seventh place on occasion.

We did another thing as well. The results of these surveys were tied into the superintendents' bonus system. The better the ratings the better chance of receiving a higher bonus. Even this did not always work. Some of the older superintendents were unresponsive to these new methods. They believed that if it was good enough before, then it was good enough now.

Continuing to monitor progress is an essential element in being a great builder. You cannot expect to rely on outdated methods and designs just because they worked before. Commitment to the past is like having a balloon and expecting it to never lose air. Before you know it, the balloon is flat and the competition has passed you up.

Keeping track of all progress and reading it closely will prevent larger problems down the road. We monitored all progress and created charts to indicate increases or decreases in our product and personnel acceptance. One project showed signs of a conflict arising between the customer and customer service. Although the project was covered by a very competent service person, the personality of the service person and the customers was getting to a sharp point.

Changing that person caused concern, but the service person accepted the outcome because it had nothing to do with his ability to perform the job. The new service person was welcomed by the customers and the problem was overcome before it could fester.

Most builders do not have the ability or the manpower to perform this kind of survey and deal with the results to this extent. However, turning the other way when these things are obvious is not the way it should be handled either. As I have mentioned several places before, the builder knows little about really building and even less about the customer and usually finds himself in trouble well after the fact.

If a builder doesn't care what you think about their product or service a year after you purchased, then you probably purchased from the wrong builder. However, you need to find this out before you buy. How? Check with existing owners as to their opinion of the builder. Check with the city or county agency that has the most contact with the builder. Just remember that the builder pays large sums of money to that agency for the privilege of building and only the customer pays the builder. Look at other builders' projects and compare the quality and price. Keep in mind that gingerbread doesn't count and walk their production homes if you can, since models are designed to turn your head and not assure you of what you will get. If you have access to a survey, read it carefully. Many may be paid-for advertisements. Those that are pictured in a builder's ad are generally paid or somehow reimbursed for their time. Also, don't expect a negative survey ever to be made public.

Implementing Corrections—

I would have to say that basically every builder I've met or worked for are reasonably intelligent. They generally have a higher degree of learning than most in the business. They usually are polished enough to compete with used car salesmen. They have style and mannerisms that set them apart from others.

However, what they learned in school is business and finance. Most don't know what end of the hammer to pick up to say nothing about a paint brush. They generally have a superior attitude and look down on those they hire. Their solutions are always right and most of the time your opinion doesn't count. They can speak in front of hundreds at a builder get-together but be deathly afraid of one lonely customer.

Many builders are oblivious to the proper method of implementing corrections. Their first choice is to fire the person involved and get someone else to replace them. Their second choice is to give the order to change and then consider the problem solved. They feel they have given enough time to this problem and now that the order has been given—it's on to bigger and better things.

I have been blessed to work for several companies that operated differently. The Konwiser Corp. and The William Lyon Company were the only two that truly operated differently.

The William Lyon Company was the epitome of a well run company. One that not only knew changes needed to take place, but wanted you to make those changes for the good of the entire company. They gave you the tools and the empowerment to make those changes and would give you more, if needed.

The Konwiser Corp., being the smaller of the two, had tighter policies. You were expected to make changes, but you probably best run it by the boss first. The eyes over the shoulder method of being the boss were generally not noticeable. However, you normally had to report your moves at some point in time.

Items that need correction cannot remain uncorrected for any length of time. Situations have a way of changing or the facts become blurred or the need to implement the correction fades away. To correct and then put the problem behind you is an absolute must.

Some builders I have known have a tendency to let things slip for fear of offending the party involved and letting these offences pile up until the least little thing sends them off the deep end. The bad thing about this is that the offending party feels he's been wronged and not the other way around.

If that builder could have come to grips with a proper correction, he would have had a more productive worker and possibly eliminated the firing process. Of course, this only works if the builder really knows how to implement the correction. If it's a shouting match, then it's the wrong approach. If it can be discussed quietly and reasonably you have reached a new level in that worker's eyes. You will benefit from the improved working relationship for years to come.

Rewarding Excellence—

This could be the hardest part for some builders to do—rewarding excellence. The method of how it is done is as important as what is done.

The two afore mentioned companies, The William Lyon Company and The Konwiser Corp. did this better than any other company I know. The rewards, of course, were relative to their size in the industry. This has to be kept in mind when you think you should get a big bonus from a small company. It generally doesn't happen.

I received many *surprises* from TKC. Bonuses for the jobs, for Christmas, trips, appliances, events, 401K, project partnerships, etc., were sometimes mysteriously given out with no explanation, but welcomed none the less. I felt honored even when the amounts were less than the year before. I understood that in order to receive the company needed to *make*.

The William Lyon Company was a real life saver by all meaning of the words. Without the General keeping his word, and mind you that was all we had between us, I would probably still be driving down the freeway during rush hour to some office to put in a full days work. He may have no idea how grateful I am that he felt obligated to fulfill a promise even when the banks were knocking down the front door.

We had bonuses for what we did, what the superintendents did, how well the company did, Christmas, trips, plus 401Ks, etc., and there didn't seem to be an end to what he was willing to give as rewards.

Some of the amounts were exceptional and by investing that properly, I was able to retire a number of years later.

The programs for the workers were also exceptional. Not only did the monetary rewards pour forth, but public recognition was also a reward. To be truly honored by your peers, as well as the general public, is a great feeling and generally lasts longer than the money.

Rewards don't always have to be in the form of money. Although this is always well received, many times just recognition of a job well done or the proverbial pat on the back will do. Just to have the boss recognize your efforts, especially to others, will live with the worker for a long time.

Our division at the Lyon Company started by portraying the winning superintendents, assistants and customer service personnel's, picture on a professional plaque within sight of all people in the division. Also an accounting was displayed as to who won the previous times as well as who won for the entire year.

These winners were proud to be displayed in the office. They knew what they won it for and how much hard work it took to win the prize. They didn't go around boasting, but you could see that the other division personnel envied this recognition.

The other division in our main office soon started their own program. This was the division that got up to seventh place (occasionally) on the survey ratings and had trouble really following the General's direction. They started this program after complaints from their workers began to mount.

We would also give the local newspaper an article describing the award and sometimes we even got in a picture or two.

But, no matter how much you do for "public consumption" it also has to be done in private. To treat these hard working employees honestly and with respect is the hardest thing to do. If you're the boss, the tendency is to issue orders and be on your way. Not caring about what problems they may be up against or knowing all the circumstances will undercut all your public utterances.

It's true that by hiring the best you can find they should be able to figure out what to do in almost any situation. That may not be their problem. Theirs may be trying to figure the boss out. One day it's to be done this way and the next—that way. A person who wants to please and do his (her) best may be wrong both days.

I've had that *"dammed if you do and dammed if you don't"* situation many times. One employer used to change his mind whenever it suited him. It was exceedingly hard to follow his thoughts at times. If he was in a good mood, you did things right. If a bad mood prevailed—watch out.

I had another employer that used to criticize everything I did. It got to the point I was really frustrated and asked him if there was ever anything I have done right for him. "Oh of course," came the reply. Then he went right on criticizing my work. His criticism wasn't the helpful kind. It was meant to demean you and make you look stupid.

This is the same builder that refused to have me order some wood window frames—like the plan called for and told me to have the rough carpenter fix it so we didn't need them. We soon parted ways. I just couldn't work for a company that didn't seem to have any moral standards.

Proper treatment of employees leads directly to what the public feels about the company. If your employee feels needed and appreciated, then so will the customers. After all—the customer is the ONLY one that pays the builder. All others take the builder's money.

This kind of treatment applies to any company. It also applies to your gardener, grocery clerk, mail person, meter reader, your neighbor, etc., etc. We are all each others customers, whether we want to be or not.

When this is done, the rewards are many.

Press "*" To Be Ignored—

Awhile back, I came across an article in the Reader's Digest that fit right in with my slant on customer service. It had to do with phone trees, or as some of you know it by— press a button and take your chances.

Over the last few years, being able to talk with a real live person to help resolve your problem has become a rarity. Now you have to decide which option you need to use to come close to satisfying your needs. Of course, none of the options really pinpoint your problem, so you have to make a guess. Naturally your guess is usually wrong and you have to start all over.

Usually you start marking down the possible choices as they are being announced. Now you may end up with more than the one you really want and still have to make a choice; the wrong one—usually.

Now you try an option that wasn't mentioned. Pressing "0" for the operator has in the past been answered with a real live voice. However, some companies are ignoring this request for several tries before finally answering. It's, apparently, some kind of punishment for calling them in the first place.

"Customer service has become a war when it should be a cooperative venture," says Lauren Weinstein, consumer advocate and co-founder of the group People For Internet Responsibility.

This is not to say that all phone trees are set up badly. I would much rather talk with a good phone tree than to have my request forwarded on to the Philippines or India. At least the phone tree person is fairly easy to understand and usually doesn't have a heavy accent.

If these companies, which insist on making customer service a mine field of horrors, would only call themselves and pretend they have a problem, they would see the frustration that builds up in their once proud customer. This is the customer that the company has spent many dollars on to make a customer in the first place and is now about to lose them just to save money. These companies still haven't learned that *"good customer service doesn't cost—it pays."*

I must mention another form of service provided for the customer. This is the "live—online" service that allows you to talk with someone and have a problem resolved. I believe that most of us would rather talk to a computer than to an individual. That way they may never know how stupid you may be.

I must admit that I was skeptical at first when I was offered this feature. After all, I was having problems with my computer getting connected to the internet so how could I talk with someone online?

I had recently signed up with *Verizon* for their DSL service. It had just recently become available in my area and it was professed to be so much faster than dial-up. It also cost the same, so why shouldn't I try it?

Everything was going fine for the first week or so and then on day it just wouldn't connect me to the internet. Then this option popped up to talk with a service rep online. I put my question in and waited for something to happen. It said that it may take several minutes before a rep would be with me. Many, many minutes later, still nothing. I went to my original plan of using a phone to communicate directly.

After about forty-five minutes, the problem was solved. Somehow something in my computer changed and kicked the settings off.

This Verizon service rep was very nice and was able to talk me through to the right solution. I actually had been online, but my computer wouldn't show anything. However, the reason that no one answered my online call was never given.

Several weeks later the same thing happened. I again used their online request and heard nothing back. I had decided to wait until the next day and try again. After all, you can only stand so much frustration before you need to step away and forget it for awhile. I started it up the next morning and after about ten minutes a pop-up massage came saying that a service rep. was ready to talk about my problem.

Again, I thought I had an internet connectivity problem, but then how did this message come up if I wasn't online?

I explained the problem and the rep. asked several questions. I answered them all and then she said to unplug all the wires on the back of the DSL modem, restart my computer and then plug everything back together. This took about three minutes and lo and behold—it worked. I don't quite know how unplugging and re-plugging an appliance can fix it, but it did. Apparently, it resets something back to normal and starts working again.

I let her know that I thought she was the smartest person on the earth and was very thankful that I didn't have to go through another forty-five minutes of trying one thing after another.

I believe this to be a case for good customer service. The previous forty-five minute session was also good customer service, but this was even several notches above good.

I know that there are many companies that want to provide good customer service. There are also many companies that have no idea of how to provide good customer service. Take for instance;

Vista Print is a printer that does its business on line. I sent them an email one day and didn't get an answer. About a week later, I received an email apologizing profusely about their tardy response, but apparently, they had been having trouble with their systems and couldn't respond. This was the perfect way of handling this situation. Instead of forgetting it altogether, they let me know they had a problem and now that it was fixed, they wanted to answer my question. I will be more receptive to their products because of their positive, pro-active actions.

I had previously mentioned that I had sent an email to General Electric and never received a response. Apparently, I wasn't a big enough person to warrant a response.

Several weeks before my GE encounter, I had sent an email to Channel 7—ABC here in Los Angeles. I had noticed that a very popular weatherman wasn't making his normal appearance and I was concerned, since their main weatherman had just come back from the hospital.

I never heard back and then one evening I happened to be watching something on CBS when this weatherman appeared to give a blurb on the upcoming weather forecast. I guess that there were some contractual problems or just a parting of the way. Channel 7—

ABC apparently didn't want me to switch over to CBS to see the weather map so they figured that if they didn't tell I might not find out. I lost a lot of respect for ABC once I found out.

I like Channel 7's weather better than the other majors but right now there doesn't seem to be that much difference that I can't be satisfied with the others. That's what happens when goofs are made for the wrong reasons.

Most companies are afraid to tell the customer the truth. They feel that a white lie won't hurt, or a deceptive answer is best for all concerned. This sounds like the way a politician would respond. We've all heard too many of those kind of answers. We don't need any more.

Conclusions—

This book is not meant to be critical of all companies that have customer service. As you have read, some large companies that could afford to give great service—don't and some small companies that really can't afford it—*do*. Many companies really try, but fail miserably. Some companies don't really try and succeed in bringing great customer service to their customers.

You will find that the people in charge of these companies are the direct link to customer service succeeding or failing. They are the ones that set the tone of how the company is to be run. They determine the staffing needs and the policy setting practices of the company. There isn't anyone else that can be blamed for bad service.

There are times when a good CEO sets the right policies and the company fails to carry them out, resulting in bad service. Then the CEO needs to step in and make things right. The offending party(s) needs correcting or replacing. The customer needs an apology and whatever else is warranted to satisfy the customer. The CEO should never be too big to say SORRY. Customers generally understand when a heart-felt apology is given and start immediately to gain, again, respect for the company.

This philosophy not only pertains to the building industry, but to every company that wants our business. If you ever run across a company that snubs the customer—*that company is not worthy to stay in business.* If at all possible, you should take your business elsewhere. Even if the next company is priced higher, you will be money ahead in the long run.

You may also be frustrated, when dealing with larger companies, knowing that you just can't buy the product you need someplace else. So you feel you have to put up with bad service. Nothing could be further from the truth. Most people feel that the company is so big that a complaint would never reach the right people to do any good. So they suffer through the bad service.

You **must** voice your feelings anyway you can. Whether it's writing a letter, sending an email or just voicing your opinion to the retailer that sells the product, you must let your feelings be known. Your comments will reach the right people—maybe after some time, but they will be heard.

That some time may be when the CEO is trying to figure out why the company is loosing money or the product name is dwindling or another company has taken over their spot in the market. You can rest assured that something will happen.

Never say that it is too much bother to complain about bad service. If you don't say something, more people will suffer and maybe you will be snubbed again. "If only I would have said something last time…" will be your answer.

Of course, we must all realize that we are each others customers. Therefore it wouldn't be fair for you to come un-glued every time something goes wrong. However, you can complain in a *positive* manner. Letting the company know that they seem to be having a problem in a certain area and maybe offer a suggestion or two. Positive remarks are generally taken positively. Harsh, negative and demeaning remarks are pointless and act negatively on gaining any results. Many times you can place yourself in the customer service reps. shoes and see how you would react. If you feel that they are concerned about your problem and seem to be looking for an answer, this is the time to help them find it.

I also understand that there is some value in blowing off some steam. I've done it many times and it has a therapeutic effect that just can't be found elsewhere. I used to have a sub-contractor that was always on the receiving end of my wrath. It wasn't like he didn't deserve it. His company used to have two schedules that they would impose at the same time. The first one was for the installation of their wrought iron and then schedule the very next day to go back and fix it. I let the owner know that I wasn't blasting away at him, but rather his company that screwed up so often. He understood and actually welcomed my tirades. It was a really good stress releaser for me and we still remained friends. He once said that if I didn't call, he more than likely was out of a job. He was a good sub-contractor.

Mission Statements
(May be used without prior permission)

It is the goal of the Customer Service Department to give the very best service to all its customers and to do so in a professional manner and willing spirit

It is our duty to provide the very best service to all our customers

All persons that we come in contact with are considered our customers and deserve the very best in service

Our goals with all our customers are to make you feel *Welcome, Important, Understood and Appreciated.*

The quality of the relationship is as important as the quality of the product

Your complete satisfaction with your home is our main goal in customer service

Quality + Team Work + Attitude = Customer Satisfaction

Our customer service goals in Product, Performance and Personnel are to exceed all expectations, *including yours*

Great customer service doesn't cost—it PAYS

To dispel an old tale that, "the customer is always right"— I would like to say that it just isn't so.

BUT—the customer is always the customer

Thanks for allowing me to speak to you about customer service. Please remember that we are all customers to each other and we need to treat everyone accordingly.

Ron

HF   Are You Being
5415.5   Served Yet? Customer
B474   Service Evolution /
2006

HF   Are You Being
5415.5   Served Yet? Customer
B474   Service Evolution /
2006

DATE DUE

Return Material Promptly

Printed in the United States
70831LV00002B/52

9 781424 124855